# HANDMAID TO THEOLOGY

## AN ESSAY IN PHILOSOPHICAL PROLEGOMENA

### WINFRIED CORDUAN

#### FOREWORD BY NORMAN L. GEISLER

WIPF & STOCK · Eugene, Oregon

Wipf and Stock Publishers
199 W 8th Ave, Suite 3
Eugene, OR 97401

Handmaid to Theology
An Essay in Philosophical Prolegomena
By Corduan, Winfried
Copyright©1981 by
ISBN 13: 978-1-60608-840-1
Publication date 6/3/2009
Previously published by Baker Book House, 1981

*To June*

# Contents

# Foreword

This book is a most needed and creative beginning in theological prolegomena. It utilizes both traditional and novel constructs in the attempt to reestablish the rightful role of philosophy as the handmaid of theology. For this task the author is highly qualified. His extensive background in theology and philosophy provides an excellent basis for his explorations. This work is a step toward remedying evangelical theology's long-time neglect of philosophy. But despite the author's rightful insistence on the need for philosophical constructs in doing systematic theology he does not buy uncritically or unnecessarily into any philosophical system. The author's presuppositions are thoroughly evangelical. His work provides evident proof that philosophically sophisticated evangelicals are capable of bringing the results of their intellectual labors into the practical service of evangelical theology. Refreshing is the author's unflinching rejection of the all-too-popular myth that nothing of much help to contemporary theology can be found in ancient or medieval thinkers. Such blind identification of contemporaneity and truth has, in our opinion, led many otherwise good theologians into obscure and even unorthodox cul-de-sacs. Particularly helpful to those whose forte is biblical theology is the emphasis on the need to use concepts compatible with the Bible when constructing a systematic theology. This book turns over new ground in theological prolegomena. Its pacesetting insights signal a return to a proper harmony between philosophy and biblical theology in the practice of systematic theology among evangelicals.

Norman L. Geisler

# Preface

This work may very well accomplish its purpose, even if no one will be convinced of all of the specific points in it. Its major goal is to facilitate discussion on its central theme: the inevitable reliance of theology on certain philosophical concepts. All too frequently the theological task is carried on without taking the proper philosophical roots into account, whether they be from first-century or twentieth-century thought. And in particular, the theologians in the evangelical tradition, who are specifically addressed in this volume, many times obscure or ignore the distinction between biblical theology and systematic theology. This work is intended as a tool to call attention to the need for serious philosophical thinking by the theologian. If such thinking should result, even in the form of a point-by-point refutation of each of my arguments, my writing will not have been in vain.

It is from this vantage point that the novel conception of prolegomena adopted in this book is to be understood. Who has ever heard of a work in prolegomena addressing a topic such as regeneration? Traditionally, prolegomena constitutes an introduction to theology. In works in systematic theology it will be the first part or chapter, dealing with preliminary matters before one can proceed to the actual theologizing. Likewise, in academic courses in

theology prolegomena may consist of the introductory
philosophical material of which we must dispose before
we can delve into the actual content of revelation.
However, such an understanding of prolegomena rests
on a misconstruing of the role of philosophy in theology.
Philosophy permeates systematic theology. The theologian cannot ever get away from the fact that philosophical
thinking is an integral part of the way that we understand
and disseminate revealed truth. Certain philosophical
points need to be made prior to beginning actual theology.
But that does not mean that once they are made we are
done with philosophy. On the contrary, wherever we turn
in theology, we are confronted with the need for clear
philosophical categories. Thus even when we enter the
arena of soteriology we have not outgrown the need for
philosophy.

This book is intended to rehabilitate philosophy to her
proper role as handmaid to theology. But theology, the
alleged queen of the sciences, must understand that she
is dependent on the handmaid. Hence we must keep from
seeing anything demeaning to philosophy in this metaphor. In fact, one could be so bold as to say that it implies
a certain amount of conceptual priority for philosophy.

Probably not since the Hellenistic era has philosophy
been represented by as many schools as it is today. Whenever one openly identifies with a particular school, one
has automatically become vulnerable to critiques from all
other schools. I have found the conclusions of Thomistic
philosophy most helpful in coming to terms with many
of the problems under consideration in this book. But I
may plead in my own behalf that mine is not an uncritical
acceptance. What the reader will find here is not thir-
teenth-century thought, but twentieth-century philosophy
making use of the rich heritage of the past. Thomas Aquinas does not stand unscathed in this essay; next to him
the person most often cited with approval is the contemporary transcendental Thomist, Karl Rahner. It would be

a shame for this piece of writing, as for any other, if it were dismissed simply because of the general category into which it falls rather than because of the specific points it makes.

A question this book seeks to address both implicitly and explicitly, but not definitively, is to what extent the theologian has flexibility in choosing his philosophical groundwork. Clearly some conceptualizations are superior to others. And regardless of which concepts we use, certain notions need to stand inviolable, for example, the creaturehood of man and the deity of Christ. But one cannot dictate to one's culture how to express those truths, if the culture is devoid of one's favorite philosophical concepts. Thus it is imperative that we keep in mind the contingency of all philosophical formulations. The conclusions I draw here are most fitting for the intellectual milieu in which I am operating; it is my hope that a sufficient number of people share this milieu so that I am not speaking to myself. But even though I maintain that this is the best word in philosophical prolegomena, I certainly have no illusions of its being the last word. In fact, as a stimulus to dialogue, it must be superseded.

This point is an important one to make in our day of increasing cultural awareness. There is much talk about cross-cultural contextualization. Different people think and talk with different concepts, and a theology which does not take this difference into account will quickly lose its audience. A prolegomena very different from this one may need to be written for a third-world country. But there are two *sine qua nons* which must be observed: a different prolegomena must nonetheless be as faithful to revealed data as this one seeks to be, and contextualization may never proceed at the price of thoughtfulness and rigor.

No book such as this one can be produced without drawing on the resources of many people: the thoughts of many teachers and writers, the interest and support of colleagues and friends, and the small, yet vital, helps rendered to me here at Taylor University. Thanks must go to my students, Miss Cheryl L. Cashner and Mr. Thomas E. Heard, for preparing the index in record time. I want to particularly thank Norman L. Geisler, whose willingness to write a foreword and to provide helpful suggestions is only one of many ways he has supported me over a number of years. My sons, Nicky and Seth, may be pleased that, at least for a while, Daddy will not be typing on the book. But, as must be the case for so many people working on books, my largest thanks must go to my wife, June, to whom this book is dedicated. During the many long evenings of writing, the "handmaid" must have appeared as an upstart rival to her.

# 1

# What Is Prolegomena?

The word *prolegomena* is derived from a Greek participle meaning "the things which are spoken before." Traditionally in an academic setting a "prolegomena" has been considered to be a preparatory study laying down basic principles or the groundwork for further exploration of a particular discipline. Its goal is not to reach final conclusions, but by its very nature it may delimit the extent and kinds of conclusions that can be reached. At times a prolegomena may be an intentional revision of basic presuppositions in order to move a whole field in a new direction.[1]

This study is a prolegomena to systematic theology. As such it examines the presuppositions underlying theology. It is a transcendental enterprise in that it asks the question, "What are the philosophical conditions which make theology possible?" This examination is based on three assumptions.

1. Systematic theology is a given. We shall nowhere in this work attempt to prove the reality of theology either as a discipline or, less trivially, as a meaningful endeavor. Nor will we pass judgment on particular conclusions of

[1]This was done by Immanuel Kant with his *Prolegomena to Any Future Metaphysics* (Indianapolis: Bobbs-Merrill, 1950).

theology if that is avoidable. Instead we will begin with
the conclusions of theology and try to discover the philosophical presuppositions and categories which go into
determining the content. (By "theology" we mean here
the exposition of divine revelation. "Philosophy" in contrast refers to all forms of rational analysis and speculation.)

This methodology does not intend to assume, except
heuristically, that somehow theology describes a set of
indisputable facts about which all theologians are in
agreement. Nothing could of course be further from the
truth. It often appears that there is nothing on which all
theologians (meaning by that term professional practitioners of theology) are in harmony. But it is precisely at
this point that philosophical prolegomena becomes interesting and worthwhile. For it is frequently the case that
the very disagreement is due to differing philosophical
backgrounds.

In the light of the theological diversity, this study has
to be primarily devoted to one type of theology; we will
restrict ourselves to what is variously known as classical,
orthodox, or evangelical theology. Even here there is no
unanimity of course. But we do have a consensus on many
important points of doctrine.[2] This is not to say that we
may not find ourselves using insights from thinkers outside of the evangelical theological camp where those are
helpful. But in the main, and without apology, we will be
preparing a prolegomena for traditional orthodox
theology.

2. The fact of philosophical presuppositions to theology
is a given. We will not try to present lengthy arguments

[2]Included in this list of agreed-upon doctrines are the deity and humanity
of Jesus Christ, the inspiration of the Bible, the necessity of the atonement
for salvation, etc. This list will clearly cut across denominational and confessional lines. It embraces not only traditional Protestant divisions, but is
appropriate to varying degrees to Roman Catholic and Eastern Orthodox
contexts as well.

to the effect that any theology is predicated on a prolegomena, either tacit or explicit, though this is our contention. Support for this proposition will be plentiful as we proceed through this project. We will let the accumulated examples which we will harness speak for themselves. In addition, we shall make some more general comments on this proposition when we look at the nature of systematic theology.

3. Philosophical prolegomena is not trivial. A brief look at the history of Christian thought should suffice to convince us of the truth of this proposition. Without getting ahead of ourselves, let it simply be said at this point that some of the most vehement controversies concerning Christian doctrine, for example, the disputes about Christology or the Eucharist, have their origin to a large extent in differing philosophical starting points of the disagreeing parties.

**Prolegomena and Related Disciplines**

We can clarify what we mean by prolegomena by comparing and contrasting it with three other forms of philosophical inquiry. All three deal with subject matter similar to that of prolegomena, but differ in important respects which make prolegomena a unique endeavor.

1. *Prolegomena is not philosophy of religion.* Prolegomena often makes use of philosophy of religion, but the two disciplines are by no means identical. Philosophy of religion stops short of theology. It is possible to "do" philosophy of religion without any regard for the conclusions of systematic theology. This is evidenced by the fact that many philosophers who have virtually no commitment to any Christian theological proposition nevertheless are active practitioners of philosophy of religion. In fact, some thinkers attempt to use philosophy of religion to demolish Christian truth-claims.

In contrast, prolegomena is an "in-house" affair. As

mentioned above, it is based on the (at least heuristic) acceptance of the conclusions of theology and tries to uncover its presuppositions. Thus it is committed to an analysis of theological content as given; this content is outside of the domain of philosophy of religion. Some religions recognize no theology per se. Such is the case with Hinduism, for example. Consequently, it is not possible to speak of a Hindu prolegomena. Nonetheless, there is such a thing as a Hindu philosophy of religion since there are typically Hindu philosophic conceptualizations. The reason there can be no Hindu prolegomena is that Hinduism recognizes no content as conclusively proven. In contrast, within the Christian context there exists the possibility for both a philosophy of religion and a prolegomena. Despite overlap the two are not identical.

2. *Prolegomena is not apologetics.* Apologetics is the defense of Christian truth-claims. It attempts to show why Christianity is intellectually acceptable. In carrying out this task, apologetic methodologies differ. Some proceed with a step-by-step verification of various Christian claims,[3] whereas others deal with Christianity as a whole.[4] But all of these approaches have in common the goal of giving some reason for accepting the truth of Christianity.

Many of the arguments which are used in apologetics will also be found in prolegomena (just as apologetics uses philosophy of religion). But prolegomena does not have validating the truth of Christianity as its goal. It uncovers the presuppositions for accepting and understanding Christian truth.

This distinction is a subtle one. Of course prolegomena deals with truth. All rational thought ultimately does. But it does not stop with verification. It moves on to under-

[3]Cf. Norman Geisler, *Christian Apologetics* (Grand Rapids: Baker, 1976), which begins by establishing a theistic framework, and then argues for different points of belief in a logical sequence.

[4]For example, the presuppositional apologetic by Cornelius Van Til, *The Defense of the Faith* (Philadelphia: Presbyterian and Reformed, 1955).

standing. We are not merely asked to accept a point of doctrine as true (which, again, may be only an assumption), but we are given particular concepts which allow us to understand that doctrine in a particular way. Apologetics stops far short of that last step.

3. *Prolegomena is not natural theology.* Natural theology comprises a set of conclusions about God and the world based on a general revelation which God has made universally available to mankind. We contrast natural theology with revealed theology which bases itself on God's special revelation in Christ and in Scripture. Natural theology relies on information apart from those particular sources of revelation. That means natural theology becomes very philosophical, utilizing reason and common insights. Typical questions considered by natural theology are the existence of God, the nature of God, and the nature of man.[5] It deals with much of the same material as systematic theology, but with a far more restricted source of knowledge.

Insofar as natural theology is considered preliminary to systematic theology, it shares many of the questions and approaches of prolegomena. But prolegomena does not restrict itself to natural revelation. On the contrary, one of the most interesting aspects of prolegomena is the investigation of the philosophical concepts underlying our appropriation of special revelation. Prolegomena considers the philosophical background to understanding particular doctrines taught by special revelation. Thus there is a decided difference between natural theology and prolegomena.

## The Tools and Method of Systematic Theology

In order to come to terms with the nature and function of prolegomena, it will now be helpful to look at theology

[5]The epitome of a systematic natural theology may be Thomas Aquinas, *Summa contra Gentiles*, 4 vols. (Garden City, NY: Doubleday, 1955–57).

itself. We will then be better able to understand the contribution that prolegomena makes.

"Theology" is a very ambiguous word. It can refer to almost any utterance concerning Christian truth, such as a simple statement of faith. But we will use the word *theology* in its most technical sense to mean a cohesive reflection on Christianity. Thus when we talk about "theology" without further qualification, we mean that discipline usually called "systematics" or "dogmatics." We will use these three terms interchangeably.

Theology, as we want to understand it, is the end product of the work of the theologian or of the church in its teaching capacity. Or, to put this point starkly, the Christian theologian contrives a theology; it is not given to him. What is given to him is revelation, but not theology.

Revelation constitutes the theologian's starting point. We shall argue later that the Bible is the appropriate and proper locus of revelation. But we can also refer to general revelation, and, for the sake of argument, mistaken notions as to what are sources of revelation, such as the church, traditions, or visions in the night. Regardless of the locus, to lay a claim to doing Christian theology, the theologian must begin with revelation. In keeping with our self-imposed restraints, we shall from now on limit our discussion to revelation in the form of the canonical Scriptures.

It is not possible, without engaging in some form of intellectual schizophrenia, to claim acceptance of Scripture as revelation from God on the one hand, and not heed its own claims about itself on the other. The Bible clearly ascribes to itself divine origin, completeness, all-pervasiveness in scope, and truthfulness.[6] It assumes, many times over, a divine standpoint; and it consistently witnesses to that fact. Thus either the Bible is accepted by

[6]See II Tim. 3:16–17; II Peter 1:20–21.

the theologian as the inspired Word of God, and hence as supreme authority, or it is not truly accepted at all.

Clearly, then, the theologian does not begin with his own ideas, but with a propositional revelation from God. This starting point adds enormous weight to his work, both in terms of privilege and of obligation. By his call and training to be a theologian he is allowed to reflect on the grandeur and mystery of his faith in a manner sometimes not open to other believers. At the same time, his work requires him to be faithful and punctilious in the explication of revealed truth.

Now, when we speak of scriptural revelation, we realize that Scripture is extremely complicated. The Bible was written by men under the inspiration of the Holy Spirit; yet it reflects the humanity of its authors in wide-ranging ways, for example, in the style and idiosyncrasies of the individual writers, as well as in the very fact that human language is used. Furthermore, the Bible is not a systematic theology textbook which answers all our questions directly and unequivocally. Scriptural interpretation is, then, a complex process which must begin with a careful study of the written text; and theology must begin with exegesis, utilizing the historical-grammatical method of hermeneutics.

But even clear exegesis is still far removed from yielding a systematic theology. Exegesis brings us face to face with the teaching of a particular passage of Scripture. Now we need to see that passage in a twofold context. First we need to discern the place of the passage within the teaching of the book as a whole. This takes us into the realm of biblical theology. We notice that different books of the Bible tend to take on individual viewpoints. This is not to say that they contradict or disagree with each other, but that they take different perspectives and have varying emphases.

These larger units of teaching must then be viewed in the context of the theology of the Bible as a whole. This is still in the realm of biblical theology rather than systematic theology. Even though we are now dealing with universal themes and the teaching of the entire Bible, we are still not in the area of systematics. Systematic theologizing does not occur until the theologian takes the biblical theology and appropriates it to his own contemporary context. There are three reasons why this appropriation is necessary:

1. The language of the Bible is not the contemporary theologian's language. Even if one of the three biblical languages, Hebrew, Aramaic, or Greek, should be his native tongue, there would be thousands of years of linguistic development coming between him and the Scriptures. The theologian by necessity communicates in the language of his day and his environment. Repeating biblical phrases verbatim does not constitute theology. Theology can occur only when the theologian communicates the biblical phrases and content in his own linguistic context. This is not to say that every single biblical expression needs to be paraphrased before it can become part of a theological system, but many do.

2. The thought forms of the contemporary theologian differ from those of the biblical writers. Contained in the linguistic differences is a difference in concepts which the language expresses. The ancient Hebrews thought differently from the ancient Greeks, who in turn thought differently from contemporary Germans, Americans, or Chinese, all of whom also differ from each other in their thought forms. Certainly we do not want to make light of the common elements of the human experience. Nonetheless, the conceptual construction we place on our experiences may vary from culture to culture. Our cultural and conceptual context differs from that of the biblical writers.

3. The contemporary theologian asks questions different from those asked by the biblical writers. Not all his questions will be different, but even those that are the same may be expressed differently. For instance, the contem-

porary theologian may be relatively untouched by the
questions of national origin and identity posed and answered by the Jewish writers of the Old Testament, but
he may—using the same scriptural material—raise and
attempt to find answers to questions concerning provi-
dence and election which did not occur to the original
author. In this context we may not ignore almost two
thousand years of developing Christian thought. To cite
another example, when Paul wrote Colossians 1, he had
obviously never heard of the Council of Nicaea, but the
contemporary theologian utilizing that christological passage cannot but think in Nicaean terms, even if he intends
to refute the particular conclusions of that council.

Much of what is being said here will be elaborated
throughout the remainder of the book. Suffice it for now
to realize that the theologian must of necessity appropriate biblical theology to his cultural context. Different cultures do produce different theologies. To use a modern
example, there is a Black theology which differs from
other theologies because Black language, thought forms,
and concerns differ from those of other ethnic and social
groups. Of course the biblical foundation ought to be
universal.

Recognizing that theologies differ from each other because of their cultural conditions is not relativism or subjectivism. It is not relativism because the basic truth does
not change from culture to culture; only the way in which
truth is expressed and applied changes. Also it is not subjectivism because the theologian does not determine what
is truth. In fact, one of the marks of a good theologian is
that he handles truth carefully and in its appropriation
translates it as accurately as possible into his context. At
the same time we must recognize that the theologian,
being a fallen and restored human being, will reproduce
God's infinite thoughts only finitely and imperfectly. Thus
we return to our original point that we have an absolute
revelation, but not an absolute theology. Theology deals

with the Absolute, but that does not make the discipline itself, let alone the theologian, absolute any more than chemistry or the chemist becomes of necessity odiferous simply because the subject involves smelly substances. Prolegomena, then, comes into play at the transitional stage between biblical and systematic theology. Note that this is only one of several studies which are of interest at this point. Studies of culture, linguistics, sociology, and history can lead to revealing conclusions in looking at the background of a theology. In fact, recently many reductionistic studies have been undertaken which have tried to interpret theologies or theologians from the vantage point of one particular area.[7] But such studies are of little relevance to theological issues (not to mention their factual questionability). Whether a theologian was driven to certain conclusions by political or economic circumstances has no bearing on the value of his conclusions, but the philosophic concepts underlying those conclusions are always of paramount importance. Prolegomena investigates those concepts which the theologian uses in clothing the truths of revelation.

The theologian may use philosophy consciously or unconsciously. It is sometimes the case that when a theologian is confronted with a particular problem he takes direct recourse to a particular philosophical concept in order to solve the problem. If he has a substantial amount of training in philosophy, he may even deliberately follow one philosophical school in approaching all of his theology.

But a theologian will also use philosophy unconsciously. It is impossible to be a thinking member of one's society and not reflect the philosophical commitments of that society. And every society is governed by certain philosophical principles, even if they remain tacit. In America the dominant traits are pragmatism, empiricism, and in-

[7]E.g., Erik H. Erikson, *Young Man Luther: A Study in Psychoanalysis and History* (New York: Norton, 1958).

dividualism, whereas Germany still has not separated itself from the idealistic mind-set. It is no surprise that these philosophical inclinations should become evident in the structuring and argumentation of American and German theologies.

It is of no use to decry philosophy as being of human origin and, therefore, counterproductive to Christian theology, which is based on divine revelation. To avoid using philosophy is simply impossible. When the apostle Paul warned the Colossians against philosophy (Col. 2:8), he was alerting them against philosophy which is not in subjection to Christ. By making this statement Paul was of course already engaged in philosophy, but it was a right philosophy, one which did not infringe on the truths of Christianity. In the same way, the theologian who is conscious of his use of philosophy can adjudicate between those concepts which lend themselves to a proper expression of revelation, and those which are poor vehicles of Christian truth. But to ignore the presence of philosophy in theology leaves one blind to the possibility that one may be trying to construct a theology with very poor building blocks.

## Prolegomena as a Separate Discipline

From one standpoint prolegomena attempts to do something impossible. It tries to abstract the conceptual framework of a discussion without taking the content into consideration. Such a thing can clearly not be done. It would also be a fruitless project, except for one interested in purely abstract arguments.

What we are trying to do is less ambitious, but also more interesting from a theological perspective. Prolegomena itself is not to be confused with the content of a theology, but it does influence the content. We shall look at the philosophical concepts then, and analyze them, not

apart from the content, but to describe how the concepts
mold or even determine the content.

Such a project is possible and fruitful. The method will
frequently be comparative; that is, it will show how different philosophies have led to different theologies. This
part of our analysis will point out one reason for the no-
torious disagreements among theologians: they begin with
differing philosophical presuppositions.

But in addition to a descriptive, comparative study, we
shall raise some basic questions with regard to prolegomena. Not every philosophy is equally congenial to the truths
of theology, and we need to judge between these philosophical vehicles. This task poses a serious problem. How
much of a role should a concept of philosophical "truth"
be allowed to play? Is there one system in philosophy
which is true, whereas all others are false? If so, then only
the true one can be a serious candidate for providing a
philosophical hermeneutic. Or do many different philosophies compete with each other as to which is the best,
the most adequate, or the most expeditious, for any given
theology?

We shall work with the assumption that the truth lies
somewhere between these two extremes. For the theologian the question has to be which philosophy is most adequate in expressing a point of revelation, for in his view
revelation must always have priority over philosophy. At
the same time, a theologian can certainly not mix contradictory philosophies simply in order to have a smooth
eclectic foundation for his further thoughts. Moreover, the
issue of truth cannot be ignored either. An absurd philosophical notion may not be used to help out in theology,
no matter how convenient it might be. And it must also
be recognized that certain philosophical systems seem inherently inimical to expressing revelation, for instance,
one which denies the possibility of revelation.

This introductory chapter has of necessity been very

general. The issues are too complicated to skip ahead and cite particular points as quick examples. But now we can begin to become specific by delineating prolegomena in earnest and with details.

# 2

# Prolegomena

## *The Starting Point*

As we begin the study of prolegomena in earnest, it would seem most appropriate to define the starting point of this discipline, as we would do with any other discipline. However, as obvious as this step may appear at first glance, a second look may raise doubt as to its sensibleness. Although we are pursuing prolegomena as a unique discipline, we recognize nonetheless that it does not stand by itself. On the contrary, we have characterized it as a hermeneutic of theology and as a transcendental quest in which, given theological content, we are exploring the philosophical concepts under which the content is organized. But the concepts do not exist in themselves apart from the content. And if there are no independent concepts, there can be no starting point for prolegomena. All that prolegomena can do is to follow theology point by point and to discover the philosophical notions behind each particular point. Thus there can be no talk of a "starting point."

There are two responses to the contention that prolegomena has no starting point. First, this contention is premised on a very particulate view of philosophy. It may be necessary to operate in piecemeal fashion in order to find out in retrospect the particular philosophical presuppositions a given theologian has brought to his work. Yet assuming the basic rationality of the theologian, his intent to write coherently, and the faculty to discern patent inconsistencies, it does not seem to be an unreasonable conclusion that, when all of the philosophical puzzle pieces are put together, there emerges something of a "system" which stands behind his theology as the operating hermeneutic. And such a system, regardless of how loosely or tightly it may be envisioned, would surely have a starting point.

Secondly, as we stated earlier, prolegomena is definitely a transcendental discipline, but as such it is not totally without normative force. We argued in the first chapter that it is possible to distinguish between different philosophies as to their suitability as bearers of revelation. To carry this a step further, it is also possible to consciously choose one philosophy, presumably the one regarded as best, and to use it as the hermeneutic of a theology. In that case we can make use of the starting point for that philosophical system as the starting point for prolegomena.

This chapter examines the question of the best starting point for a philosophical prolegomena. In keeping with the preceding observations, we can apply this question both to existing theologies and to a quest after an ideal philosophical hermeneutic.

At this point it is necessary to specify what in particular we mean by "starting point." It may with good cause be disputed whether it is even possible to clearly identify a starting point for most philosophies. Do we mean a crucial premise, the historical roots, the underlying method, or perhaps something else when we speak of starting point? For general purposes many different concepts could be considered to be the starting point of a philosophy. But when in this volume we speak of the starting point of prolegomena, we have something specific in mind. It has to do with the question of whether prolegomena must follow the order of dogmatic theology, which begins with revelation from above, that is, from God. Must prolegomena start with the notion of a divine revelation, or should it start with man and the possibility of receiving revelation? To phrase the question differently, using theological jargon, should prolegomena be theocentric or anthropocentric, or, should it be carried out "from above" or "from below"? Before answering this question, let us look at two examples: Karl Barth, who carries out prolegomena "from above," and Karl Rahner, who starts out "from below."

## Karl Barth: Prolegomena from Above

The second section of the introduction to Karl Barth's imposing *Church Dogmatics* is entitled "The Task of Prolegomena to Dogmatics." In the first part of this section he discusses the need for and nature of prolegomena.[1]

In establishing his concept of prolegomena, Barth distinguishes himself from several alternatives which he considers to be inadequate. First of all he rejects the conception of prolegomena as apologetics or "eristics," to use Emil Brunner's term. In this view prolegomena consists of a preliminary defense of the possibility and truth of Christianity against the unbelief of this age. Those who advocate this position stress that nowadays Christianity has lost its credibility, and that there is no sense in proceeding with the content of dogmatics proper until the ground has been cleared for its acceptance. Barth dismisses this idea of prolegomena for three reasons.

First, according to Barth, this kind of prolegomena assumes that a general revelation precedes special revelation, and that a rejection of general revelation needs to be countered prior to any other theological work. But, says Barth, this idea is faulty because it somehow sees a rejection of general revelation as more serious than a rejection

---

[1]All of the following discussion is taken from Karl Barth, *Church Dogmatics*, I. 1, trans. G. T. Thomson (Edinburgh: T. & T. Clark, 1936), pp. 26–47.

of special revelation, when in fact the far more serious problem is the rejection of actual Christian truth.

Second, eristics loses sight of the task of theology, namely, to express the content of revelation. Barth claims that eristics gets so wrapped up in preparing the way that it diminishes the more important point of stating theological truth.

Barth's third argument against an eristic prolegomena is based on the notion that dogmatics must be on the offensive, and that, therefore, the only viable apologetics is a declaration of revelation. He supports this idea by raising three points. (1) Faith should never take unbelief seriously. Thus it ought never to stoop to battle unbelief on its own ground or to attempt to defend itself against unbelief. (2) The task of dogmatics proper is so demanding and so much in need of further work that effort spent on an extraneous eristic prolegomena is effort misspent. (3) There is always the danger that, after someone has carried out an eristic prolegomena, he may feel that his actual dogmatics need no longer confront unbelief. Such an idea, in Barth's view, diminishes the proper role of dogmatics.

If prolegomena is not intended to speak to unbelief, states Barth, its purpose is to confront heresy, that is, doctrinal aberrations within an originally Christian context. Prolegomena must provide the ground for discerning Christian truth from falsehood masquerading as truth. Barth stresses two particular heresies, both of which are based on improper prolegomena: modernism and Roman Catholicism.

Barth sees three levels in modernism's prolegomena, which focuses on the capability of the church to undertake dogmatics. (1) Modernism's prolegomena shows that there is a religious dimension to man, so that man may assimilate faith. (2) The modernist argues that there is a concrete object of faith. (3) He delineates his methodology. None of this, of course, is part of theology proper. Thus the modernist view attempts to establish philosophical and methodological principles prior to engaging in theological content.

The Catholic view of prolegomena, according to Barth, focuses on the mediatory activity of the church. It is the Catholic understanding that theology consists of the formulations of the truths of revelation as expounded by the infallible agencies of the church. Prolegomena delimits the nature of the church and clarifies the way in which objective knowledge of revelation is tied up with the subjective interpretations of the magisterium. The objectification of revelation leads to its defusing: God is treated as being rather than as a speaking subject.

Barth rejects both the modernist and Roman understanding of prolegomena for essentially the same reason. They both rob theology of its divine starting point and character. Although these heretical views are based on different conceptions, they have this in common, that they do not recognize the freedom with which Jesus Christ is present in the church. They tie God's free revelatory activity to the contingencies of man's created existence.

But in Barth's view prolegomena must already be a part of revealed dogmatics. It must begin with the realization that Jesus Christ is the essence of the church. Therefore, prolegomena does not prepare the way for theology, but is the first part of theology itself. It does not lay groundwork for content: it already consists of content. Prolegomena, for Barth, describes the initial contact of God with man.

Thus Barth's prolegomena is his doctrine of revelation. It concerns first of all the Word of God, Scripture, as the locus of God's revelation. But then it also concerns God as He communicates Himself to man. This second concern leads Barth to the doctrine of the Trinity which epitomizes the essence of God and, therefore, the essence of God's self-disclosure.

As we can clearly see, Barth's starting point for prolegomena is identical with his starting point for theology, namely, God Himself and His revelation. This is prolegomena from above. Barth does not begin with man. Man's only place in this scheme is as the recipient of God's revelation, insofar as God speaks to and through the church. The initiative and the content both belong to God who has come down to us and is speaking down to us.

At this point we will forego a description and critique of Barth's doctrine of revelation, as interesting and apropos as that may appear.[2] For now our purpose has simply been to illustrate the basic scheme of one prolegomena from above.

## Karl Rahner: Prolegomena from Below

What we call prolegomena here Karl Rahner, the German Jesuit, calls "fundamental theology." His most explicit descriptions of this discipline are found in *Hearers of the Word* and *Foundations of Christian Faith.*[3]

Rahner clarifies what he means by fundamental theology in the introduction to *Foundations.*[4] He refers to it as the "first level of reflection." It is not the same thing as dogmatic theology, which constitutes the second level. Nowadays dogmatic theology consists of so many diverse disciplines that it is impossible to maintain expertise in all of them. Consequently we need an introduction to theology which does not consist of summarizing statements covering all of these disciplines, but which represents a basis for unifying all of theology under a comprehensive perspective.

[2]The brevity of our description is not meant to imply that there is nothing to criticize in Barth's representation of any of the views he rejects. In particular, it is questionable whether Barth even approaches doing justice to Roman Catholic theology.

[3]Karl Rahner, *Hearers of the Word*, trans. Michael Richards (New York: Seabury, 1969), and *Foundations of Christian Faith*, trans. William V. Dych (New York: Seabury, 1978).

[4]Rahner, *Foundations*, pp. 3–14. This passage serves as source for the ensuing discussion.

This perspective is provided by fundamental theology. Fundamental theology raises the basic question of the possibility of dogmatic theology. It is an attempt to correlate the two disciplines of philosophy and theology in that it examines the initial setting in which revelation comes to man. Thus fundamental theology unites philosophy and theology. At the same time it yields a certain amount of autonomy to philosophy since it allows philosophy to establish a groundwork for the possibility of dogmatics.

For Rahner the starting point of prolegomena is the point of reception of revelation—within man. Before we can get into dogmatic theology we must look to the one to whom revelation is given and who assimilates it. The basic question fundamental theology asks is: How is it possible that finite man can hear the word of infinite God?

This is not to say that Rahner is preparing the way for a humanistic theology. Nor is he somehow downplaying the central role of God or Christ in theology (whatever sense that could make). Rather he intends to clarify the locus at which God and Christ are disclosed. Revelation does not take place in a vacuum; there is a revealer and a recipient of revelation. Given that God is revealing Himself, the most basic question centers on man's appropriation of the content of revelation.

At this point we can indicate only in general terms how Rahner approaches fundamental theology. He defines man by the faculty of *potentia obedientialis*, the possibility of standing open to God.[5] Rahner considers it to be a crucial aspect of man that he has a constitutional openness to God. This is described as the "supernatural existential": "existential" because it is an important part of man's very nature, "supernatural" because it is nonetheless an

[5]Rahner, *Hearers*, pp. 53–68.

expression of God's grace.[6] Rahner goes so far as to claim
that in every instance of knowledge man implicitly makes
reference to God through a faculty of the intellect he calls
the *Vorgriff*.[7] Thus we see that for Rahner prolegomena
begins with man. Consequently here we have a prolegomena from below.

## Adjudication: Prolegomena from Above or Below?

Having looked at examples of the opposing points of
view, we now need to make a choice as to the starting
point of our prolegomena. To that end we will lay down
some basic premises.

1. *The starting point for dogmatic theology and for prolegomena need not be identical.* Theology and prolegomena
are two different disciplines, though of course intimately
related. They have different objects and methodologies.
Consequently they do not need to share the same starting
point.

This is an observation which holds true in other fields
of human knowledge as well. Frequently a particular discipline relies on another discipline. For example, psy-
chology relies on biology to some extent; biology utilizes
chemistry; chemistry nowadays makes heavy use of physics; and physics would be unthinkable without mathe-
matics. But each of these fields has its own particular
point of focus. No one would say that biology ought to
begin with the periodic table, or that chemistry should
have as its starting point the classification of living beings.

In the same way, prolegomena and systematics can

[6]Karl Rahner, "Concerning the Relationship Between Nature and Grace,"
in *Theological Investigations*, trans. Cornelius Ernst (New York: Seabury,
1961), vol. 1, pp. 297–317.
    [7]Rahner, *Hearers*, pp. 63–64. Cf. also *Spirit in the World*, trans. William
Dych (New York: Seabury, 1968), which constitutes a rather thorough description of Rahner's epistemology. *Vorgriff* is virtually untranslatable. The
attempts by Richards ("pre-concept") and Dych ("pre-apprehension") are
more likely to confuse than help.

each have their own starting points. Although they may be even more intertwined than, say, biology and chemistry, this issue is still untouched. It is true that prolegomena provides the categories for dogmatics, but that does not mean that the science of the categories itself needs to begin at the same point as the theology it facilitates.

2. *The starting point for theology is God.* The fundamental data the theologian encounters begin outside of himself. Theology has to begin with God, who has revealed Himself to man. In no other way could theology either speak with certainty or do justice to the revelation it encounters.

It is at this point that the common observation that the Bible does not attempt to prove the existence of God comes into play. The fact that God exists is assumed throughout Scripture, even in those passages which describe the ways in which God has manifested His existence. Surely the theologian has to take on a similar mind-set. His task, that of systematizing revelation, has to be predicated on the firm knowledge that there is a God and that He has revealed Himself.

Thus the theologian begins his system with the living God who is the point of origin of the entire universe. Dogmatics then must start from above. The first articles of a system must be in the intertwined areas of theology proper and revelation.

3. *Dogmatic theology renders God's revelation into human terms.* We have already elaborated this point in the previous chapter, but two truths need reemphasis here. (a) God revealed Himself to man in human terms. When God spoke, He did not speak in His language (the concept itself is unintelligible to us), but He chose to address us in our language. The Bible, which is the primary locus of revelation, is written in human historical, cultural terms. When confronting God's revelation we do not get away from human concepts, but meet the God who has revealed

Himself in them. (b) The theologian takes the revealed concepts and translates them into his concepts. Theology is the human work of coming to understand divine revelation.

4. *Prolegomena provides the human tools for handling divine revelation.* This follows from our working definition of prolegomena. Prolegomena does not define revelation; it enables the theologian to encounter it. It helps the theologian tell true formulations of revelation from counterfeit ones, and it facilitates his understanding of revelation. The point cannot be underscored enough that the theologian's standard for evaluating his work has to be, first and last, fidelity to revelation. Prolegomena merely provides a service to enable him to carry out this task. It is a necessary service, which the theologian disregards at his peril.

5. *Thus the proper starting point for prolegomena is from below, with man.* Since prolegomena is the set of human categories which are used to express divine revelation, it follows that its proper starting point is from below. We must begin with man, who he is, how he thinks, how he can receive revelation, and the concepts he employs to understand revelation. Unlike systematic theology, which must start from above, prolegomena begins from below. It is a different discipline with different, though related, goals.

### Differentiation from Barth

Since we have already indicated that Barth's prolegomena starts from above, whereas our conception is from below, our distinction from Barth seems to be rather obvious. However, a few more words of explication may yet be in order.

Part of our problem with Barth's conception of prolegomena lies with his view of dogmatic theology. We mentioned his emphasis on Scripture as the locus of God's revelation. At the risk of getting somewhat ahead of ourselves, we also need to note Barth's observation that the Word of God is not an external objective reality which confronts man. Rather it is disclosed to the community of believers, who receive it in faith.[8] Thus actually we have here an indirect view of revelation where revelation becomes explicit only upon reflection by the church, and in a significant way it is the church dogmatician who, for Barth, is instrumental in proffering revelation. There is no further criterion for distinguishing between revealed and unrevealed matter than what the church confesses. Consequently, the theologian, human being though he may be, is the only one to speak authoritatively on matters revelatory. Thus, as startling as it sounds, Barth's starting point from above is in fact located right within the church, that is, below. It is no surprise, then, that Barth does not (in fact, cannot) allow for any preparatory discipline or questions outside of the actual content of dogmatics. If the church needed to prepare herself, she would no longer be the center of revelation; and there would be a revelation apart from the church which the church would receive externally. But this does not fit Barth's scheme, where the Word of God is actualized within the church.

We can see, then, that our notion of a theology from above is different from Barth's. For Barth the starting point from above is contained subjectively within the church. We, on the other hand, posit an objective revelation from above (the Bible) which the church receives and interprets.

But even after we have said all of this, it is not clear that Barth would entirely reject our conception of prolegomena. For we are advocating neither the modernist nor the Romanist version of prolegomena. We are not trying to make theology possible through our philosophical efforts. Rather, in keeping with what we have already de-

---

[8]Karl Barth, *Evangelical Theology: An Introduction*, trans. Grover Foley (New York: Holt, Rinehart and Winston, 1964), pp. 37–47.

scribed as a transcendental method, we are accepting the
possibility, truth, and reality of theology as a given, but
then we are raising the question of the background which
has made human reflection on revelation possible. Our
quest for the categories of theology is predicated on the
existence and persistence of theological content, regardless of the efforts of the prolegomenist, theologian, or the
church as a whole. Our project is the quite modest one of
discovering the conceptual hermeneutic of theology. And,
interestingly enough, Barth indicates in at least one passage that he is not inimical to that project, though he feels
that it is the task of the philosopher and not the
theologian.[9]

*Differentiation from Rahner*

Just as we needed to clarify the distinction of our position from Barth's, it would be wrong to assume too read-
ily a complete identity between Rahner and us. Such an
identity does not exist.

It may be helpful here to bring up a distinction described by the conservative Lutheran, Helmut Thielicke.[10]
Thielicke distinguishes between Cartesian and non-Carte-
sian theology, to which he refers as type A and type B
respectively. It is his contention that type A, in which he
includes most modern and recent theology, is centered
around the assimilation of revelation. It denies the existence of revelation apart from its appropriation by the
human subject. Thus there is no content other than content as man sees it. Such a theology is inherently anthropocentric and subjective. In contrast type B posits the
objective existence of a revelation to which man may relate in varying degrees.

Rahner's prolegomena prepares the way for a theology

[9]Barth, *Church Dogmatics*, I. 1, pp. 42–43.
[10]Helmut Thielicke, *The Evangelical Faith*, trans. Geoffrey W. Bromiley
(Grand Rapids: Eerdmans, 1974), vol. 1, pp. 38ff.

of type A. For him there is no revelation apart from God's disclosure to man in transcendental subjectivity, though that process may be stretched out over the entire history of man. Throughout his writings, Rahner's method is to begin with the disclosure of God within man's subjectivity and then to reorient a particular doctrine around that transcendental starting point. Thus Rahner is locked into a kind of subjectivity which we do not want to share. For him the starting point of prolegomena has become the starting point of dogmatics. His entire theology begins from below. Such a view is very different from what we are espousing. Of necessity our philosophical categories come from below, but theology must begin from above with God's independent revelation (Thielicke's type B).

Our prolegomena begins from below, with man. The steps in our development of prolegomena will be to look at man, his nature and his receptivity to revelation; at God, as He is understood by man; and at the appropriation of some particular concepts disclosed by revelation.

# 3

# Man

*Philosophical Conception*

"What is man?" is the question that will occupy us in this chapter. More specifically, we want to determine a philosophical conception of man which does justice to the total biblical conception of man.

There certainly is no shortage of philosophical descriptions of man, as this is one of the so-called perennial questions of philosophy. There probably are as many philosophies of man as there are philosophers. This is further complicated by the fact that different philosophies come from such different presuppositions that it is no easy task to compare them. Thus it is extremely difficult to choose one as the most applicable. This choice usually has to be made within the larger perspective of a philosophical system.

Questions in philosophical anthropology cover many different areas. For example, there is the question of the basic constitution of man. There are those philosophers who hold man to be a composite of body and soul. Most celebrated among these is certainly Plato, for whom the essence of man is his spiritual nature, his soul, which is (unfortunately) for a time imprisoned in a body.[1] The same dualism appears in modified form in the thought of René

---

[1]Plato's fullest development of this idea is in the *Phaedo*.

41

Descartes.[2] Aristotle also accepts the distinction between body and soul, but for him they are always present together—the soul being the form of its material cause, the body—thus giving us man as a unity.[3] At opposite extremes on the question of the human constitution are Thomas Hobbes, who sees man as only a material entity,[4] and Bishop George Berkeley, representing the idealists for whom the material side of man is totally a function of the mental.[5]

The rub to this question comes when we realize that the issue of the composition of man is not only just one among many, but is, in the opinions of yet other philosophers, even either irrelevant or improper. For some, such as logical positivists or certain pragmatists, the entire issue is meaningless. Others believe that the issue is settled, and that far more pressing concerns require the attention of the philosopher. Among that group may be found certain materialists, for example, Karl Marx, the revolutionary,[6] and Edward O. Wilson, the sociobiologist.[7] Let these few examples suffice as illustrations of the complexity of the philosophical issues.

Someone may raise an impatient objection before we carry this discussion any further: Is there not a biblical view of man in contrast to the various philosophical ones which have been enumerated? Surely the Bible has a dis-

[2]René Descartes, *Meditations*, trans. Laurence J. Lafleur, in *Discourse on Method* and *Meditations* (Indianapolis: Bobbs-Merrill, 1960), pp. 126–43.

[3]Aristotle's fullest development of this idea is in the *De Anima*.

[4]See *The Metaphysical System of Hobbes*, ed. M. W. Calkins (Chicago: Open Court, 1905); this is a condensation of Hobbes's *De corpore*. See also T. E. Jessop, *Thomas Hobbes* (London: Longman, Green & Co., 1960), pp. 31–33.

[5]George Berkeley, *Three Dialogues Between Hylas and Philonous* (New York: Liberal Arts, 1954).

[6]Thus in the *Communist Manifesto*, where the materialism is more implicit than in some later works by Marx and Engels, e.g., Friedrich Engels, "Dialectics of Nature," in *Marx and Engels on Religion* (New York: Schocken, 1964), pp. 153–74.

[7]Edward O. Wilson, *Sociobiology: The New Synthesis* (Cambridge, MA: Harvard University, 1975).

tinctive view of man not covered by any independent philosophical analysis. In that case the only sensible procedure seems to be to uncover the biblical view of man, elaborate it, and show how it is superior to all other views. There seems to be little point in occupying ourselves with various philosophical anthropologies.

There is a lot of force to this objection. Certainly there is a biblical view of man, and this view becomes paradigmatic for the theologian. Insofar as the Bible gives us information, that becomes binding on us. But there are two reasons why our quest for a suitable philosophical anthropology has not been obviated thereby:

1. Without rehearsing all of the previous arguments, let us quickly remind ourselves of the distinction between biblical and systematic theology. Merely recounting a biblical anthropology is not sufficient for the theologian's task of couching the content of revelation in the terms of his culture. It is at this point, as we argued previously, that philosophy must come into play.

We can clarify this by indicating more specifically the direction in which we are heading. Any kind of demythologizing, as exemplified by the thought of Rudolf Bultmann,[8] is out of the question. The Bible affirms the composite nature of man with such terms as soul, spirit, body, and flesh. This is the kind of information we earlier called paradigmatic, and we cannot sweep it aside with the brush of twentieth-century modernity. Rather we must take the data and explicate them in relevant language. Here the second reason for our quest for a suitable philosophical anthropology comes into play.

2. The biblical data on man are far from unequivocal. Although the Bible uses such terms as soul and spirit, it never gives us clear definitions of them. Just to reconstruct a consistent biblical theology of these terms, one

---

[8]Rudolf Bultmann, *Kerygma and Myth*, ed. Hans Werner Bartsch (New York: Harper & Row, 1961), pp. 1–44.

has to engage in a certain amount of speculation and hy-pothesizing. And this would be assuming that the biblical usage is consistent, which in itself is questionable. Do the various Hebrew and Greek words which are translated "soul" really carry the same meaning and reference? A question such as this one cannot be answered without thorough philosophical investigation.

Moreover, all talk of myth and modernity aside, there can be no question but that the Bible does contain some references to man which we no longer find acceptable. For example, we would not say that our moral sincerity can be ascertained via a test of the kidneys (Ps. 26:2). Un-doubtedly someone will be quick to point out that this is not a case of the biblical view's being mistaken; rather, it is a matter of there being a difference between biblical and modern-day terminology. But that is not an objection. It is exactly the point we want to make: in describing man from a biblically-based point of view, there is room for a modern philosophical hermeneutic.

### Biblically Prohibited Views

As happens frequently, a good way to clarify a positive point is to differentiate it from unacceptable views. Thus the easiest way to come up with a philosophical view within a biblical perimeter may well be to note what is clearly out of bounds.

1. The Bible does not permit materialism. Although Scripture unquestionably depicts man as having a ma-terial side, there is always an immaterial side in view as well. Thus any kind of understanding of man which sees him as nothing more than a physical entity or aggregate of physical particles must be ruled out a priori.

Biblical scholars may disagree about the materiality or immateriality of all the aspects of man, particularly as presented within the Old Testament; it is not our purpose to settle this matter. But certainly the moment the Genesis account mentions that God breathed into man, an act which distinguishes man from all other creatures, man's transcendence of the merely physical becomes apodictic. A subtle variation of materialism recognizes spiritual realities (e.g., souls), but interprets them as also being material, that is, as being composed of less dense matter. Such a crypto-materialism, which is more typical of ancient thinkers than of modern ones, can be dismissed. (a) It goes contrary to the meaning of most uses of words like "spirit" and "soul," where the reference is clearly intended to be to something immaterial. (b) If spirit is crypto-material, then God is also crypto-material. Further, if God is to any extent material, and yet still infinite and omnipresent, we have either a conception of matter unacceptable to modern ways of thinking (viz., infinite matter) or a pantheistic conception of a corporal God.

2. The Bible rules out spiritualism. By spiritualism we mean here the idea that man is spiritual only, that there is no material side to him whatever. This notion is certainly counter to the biblical account of the formation of man from clay, and can thus be dismissed. This would include certain forms of idealism, namely those which deny the existence of all material reality. Eastern mysticism sometimes falls into this category. Other forms of idealism, for example, that of G. W. F. Hegel, would not be ruled out, because they only make matter subordinate to spirit.

3. The Bible rules out strict dualism. At this point we move from the obvious to the not so obvious. What we are here characterizing as strict dualism—and dismissing on a priori scriptural grounds—has been the dominant view of popular Christianity over the centuries. This can be traced to the influence of Platonic philosophy on early Christian thought.

For Plato, as for many of his predecessors (most notably the tragic mystic, Empedocles), man is his soul. This soul has, to its detriment, become entrapped in a physical body.[9] Although at present we recognize each other by our bodies on the level of our phenomenal existence, the body is actually completely superfluous to our identities and a hindrance to our personal fulfilment. This view is reflected by Plato in his theory that true knowledge can never be obtained by recourse to our (physically mediated) senses, but only by the spiritual act of recollection in which the soul recalls insights gained in previous existences.[10]

Consequently, what greater bliss could there be, particularly for the philosopher, than to free oneself from the physical prison of the body and to thrive in an exclusively spiritual state! To be disembodied is the goal of man, because matter is only a burden to bear. One's self is one's soul, and this soul must be liberated.[11]

Since this is not a work in systematic theology, but its philosophical prolegomena, we cannot here argue out all the doctrinal, let alone exegetical, relevancies. We must take recourse to a generalization which summarizes the orthodox theological position. Whereas for Plato, hope was based on the inherent immortality of the human soul, the Bible recognizes no such automatic immortality. "[God] alone possesses immortality" (I Tim. 6:16). Whatever survival after death is indicated in Scripture is the result of God's gracious act in the resurrection of the body; it is not the natural property of the human soul.

Two contrasting quotations will serve to put the difference into perspective. Plato has Socrates say in the "Phaedo":

> So long as we keep to the body and our soul is contaminated with this imperfection, there is no chance of our ever attaining to our object, which we assert to be truth.
> . . . We are in fact convinced that if we are ever to have

[9]Plato *Phaedo* 64c–67d.
[10]Ibid., 73b–76e.
[11]Ibid., 67c–d.

pure knowledge of anything, we must get rid of the body and contemplate things by themselves with the soul by itself.[12]

On the other hand, the apostle Paul states in II Corinthians 5:1–4:

> For we know that if the earthly tent which is our house is torn down, we have a building from God, a house not made with hands, eternal in the heavens. For indeed in this house we groan, longing to be clothed with our dwelling from heaven; inasmuch as we, having put it on, shall not be found naked. For indeed while we are in this tent, we groan, being burdened, because we do not want to be unclothed, but to be clothed, in order that what is mortal may be swallowed up by life. [NASB]

In short, whereas Plato longs to be free from any kind of body, Paul yearns for a new body.

What we are interested in here is not the question of what happens after death so much as the conception of man which is implied. For Plato, the essence of man is his soul apart from the body, whereas the biblical ideal is a unity of both the spiritual and corporeal components.

The Bible recognizes two dimensions to man: the spiritual side, indicated by such terms as "soul," "spirit," and "mind," and the physical side, indicated by such terms as "flesh" and "body." But these two aspects do not refer to separately existing components which are spatially connected to each other for a time, but to two elements which contribute to a unit, the human person.

### The Human Unit

Descartes sees more unity in man than does Plato. But Descartes is still a strict dualist, observing a radical di-

---

[12]Ibid., 66b, d. The translation is by Hugh Tredennick, in *The Collected Dialogues of Plato*, ed. Edith Hamilton and Huntington Cairns (Princeton, NJ: Princeton University, 1961), p. 49.

vision between body and mind. Nevertheless, Descartes tries to come to terms with the fact that mental events seem to be strictly correlated with physical events. For example, an object impinging on my arm (representing my body) may be experienced by my mind as pain, pleasure, or some other sensation. Simultaneously, my mind may command my arm to move; and the arm obeys. Thus there is causal interaction between two different realms, and a certain amount of unity has been established.[13]

There are two basic problems with Descartes's position. (1) His view implies that there is some specific physical locus at which the mind and body interact causally. But no such locus can be established. Descartes's resort to the pineal gland has become almost legendary for its being an obvious *ad hoc* grasping for straws. (2) More sharply, the whole issue of mind-body interaction in Descartes is dubious. Bodies are, in Cartesian parlance, extended substances which can be acted upon only by other extended substances. Minds are unextended substances which are immune from influence by extended substances. Therefore, mind-body interaction is already theoretically prohibited. Consequently, despite Descartes's efforts, he has still left man cleft asunder between body and soul.

On the basis of this criticism, many philosophers have opted for some refined form of materialism. At the root of recent materialism is the hypothesis (for which there is no evidence at this time) that for every mental event there is a corresponding physical event. This hypothesis has led thinkers in various directions:

1. *Eliminationism*—the theory that mental events and physical events are in effect the same, although the physical events are more fundamental. Thus talk about the mind is just ambiguous discourse which should be replaced with more lucid talk about chemical occurrences in the brain.

[13]Descartes, *Meditations*, pp. 126–43.

2. *Epiphenomenalism*—the theory that the fundamental physical processes are frequently accompanied by mental processes. These mental events, however, are nothing more than concomitant appearances. Of themselves they have no causal efficacy in influencing the body, nor do they possess any separate reality.
3. *Double-reference theories.* What the theories we are here placing under one umbrella have in common is a tenacious clinging to the integrity of mental events despite the apparent priority of the physical. Such theories, as outlined by Richard Taylor, include occasionalism, parallelism, preestablished harmony, and the double-aspect theory.[14]

Instrumental in initiating the contemporary discussion was Gilbert Ryle's *Concept of Mind.* In this book Ryle argues that Cartesian dualism along with its philosophical relatives was the result of a "category mistake." Ryle's point is that it is a mistake to put mental events in one category and physical events in another. That is, he disputes the view that mind is totally distinct from body.[15] Ryle's point appears to be a sound one. The problem is, where do we go from here? For Ryle himself mind is reduced to a certain kind of outward behavior. For many others, as we saw above, Ryle's observation has become a license to treat mental events as subordinate to the physical, while yet others have disparately ignored Ryle.

The root of all this confusion is that, even though it seems to make good sense to say that mental events constitute a category of their own, the nature of this category has not been clearly identified. Until we do so, we have no choice but to see mental events as a form of physical

[14]Richard Taylor, *Metaphysics* (Englewood Cliffs, NJ: Prentice-Hall, 1963), pp. 12–14.
[15]Gilbert Ryle, *The Concept of Mind* (New York: Barnes & Noble, 1949), pp. 15–24.

causation that is not physical, an obvious absurdity. To resolve this difficulty, we need to revive the metaphysical question of the nature of the mind or soul. Aristotle's view of the soul as the form of the body provides an alternative. For Aristotle, the form of any substance is its specification, that is, that which makes an object what it is. A cow is a cow because it has the form of a cow; a vase is a vase because it has the form of a vase; a tree is a tree because it has the form of a tree. The form is never found apart from the material in which it resides. Conversely, formless matter (prime matter) is also only a theoretical possibility. Form and matter constitute an inseparable unit. Neither the form by itself nor the matter by itself constitutes the object. Thus a vase is not merely its form nor its clay by itself, but its form and clay brought together.[16]

Aristotle applied this metaphysics to anthropology, conceiving of the soul as the form of man. Aquinas, following Aristotle, argues that what distinguishes man from animals is his intellect (man is a "rational animal").[17] Thus, on the premise that the form is what distinguishes one species from another, it is the soul, the seat of the intellectual faculties, that we must look to for the form of man. The body is physical matter distinguished from other physical matter by the soul, and the whole complex is man. Man is not the soul by itself, let alone only the body, but the entire body-soul unit.

Regarding the soul as the form of the body has several advantages:

1. This conception takes Ryle's caveat on the category mistake into consideration without falling into the trap of leaving mental events without any category of their own. It recognizes the logical distinction between mind

[16]Aristotle *Metaphysics* 1070a.
[17]Thomas Aquinas, *Summa Theologica*, I, q. 76, art. 1, in *Introduction to Saint Thomas Aquinas*, trans. and ed. Anton C. Pegis (New York: Modern Library, 1945), pp. 291–97.

and body while avoiding the strict dualism which Ryle rightly criticizes. Form and matter are regarded as distinct, each with its own logical integrity.

2. Regarding the soul as the form of the body circumvents the Cartesian problem of finding a specific physical locus for mind-body interaction. The Cartesian view was already described and criticized by Aquinas several centuries before Descartes.[18] Aquinas dismissed the idea of the soul as a "motor" which somehow drives the body it inhabits. Instead, body and soul represent an all-pervasive unity, as any form and matter do. Thus there is no question of discovering the specific locus at which or manner in which the two components exercise causality on each other. The body-soul complex is the causal unit.

3. Regarding the soul as the form of the body simultaneously allows for the physical and spiritual aspects of man. Though man is the whole, it is nonetheless possible to attribute certain properties or faculties to either his spiritual or his physical side. It is the body which eats, not the soul. It is the mind which knows, not the body. Of course the body eats at the direction of the soul, and the soul knows only by means of a sensory image (a phantasm) presented to it by the body.[19] But the difficulties which other philosophical positions encounter (e.g., with reconciling dichotomization and simultaneous interaction) are avoided with the form-matter model.

4. Most importantly, the form-matter model does justice to the biblical understanding of man. It allows for just the kind of unity in diversity which the revealed perimeter demands. The Bible's treatment of man as a whole is certainly permitted by the form-matter model, and those passages in which the Bible speaks to one of man's components can also be harmonized with this scheme without erecting illegitimate mechanical or logical compartments.

[18]Ibid., p. 294.
[19]Ibid., I, q. 84, art. 7, pp. 395–98.

Moreover, this model facilitates understanding of the sticky issue of immortality. Aquinas himself argues for the indestructibility, and therefore immortality, of the soul as a form.[20] This would permit the disembodied survival of the soul past death. However, one wonders whether Aquinas has at this point not taken an unwarranted draft at Plato's philosophical fount after all.

Of course, the form-matter model is not inimical to the view that disembodied human spirits survive past death. But this model is also most amicable to the view for which we have indicated a preference, namely, the idea of immortality through the resurrection of the body (and possibly an intermediary body prior to the resurrection). There is an acute problem here. On the one hand, we have maintained that the human person is a unity of soul and body; on the other hand, the provision of a new body seems to allow all of one's identity to reside in the soul alone between death and resurrection. And what gives us the right to affirm the identity of the postresurrection person with the preresurrection person? The skeptic Antony Flew asks facetiously why "reconstituted Flew" should be the same as "original Flew."[21]

The form-matter model can handle this difficulty with the following line of argument: (a) The form (i.e., the soul), though not identical with the man, contains the man's principle of identity. (b) It is the form which persists between separate embodiments. Let us leave it to the biblical theologians whether the correct term here is "soul," "spirit," or something else. It is also a much debated, though here inconsequential, point whether we are dealing with a brief period of disembodiment, or whether the soul is temporarily linked to an intermediary body. The important fact is that despite the physical death, the form persists. (c) Whatever matter the form resides in will take

[20]Ibid., I, q. 75, art. 6, pp. 287–90.
[21]Antony Flew, "Death," in *New Essays in Philosophical Theology*, ed. Antony Flew and Alasdair MacIntyre (London: SCM, 1955), p. 270.

on the identity provided by the form. Thus two different bodies, if they are at different times united with the same soul, will be the same person. Few thinkers, if any, would demand identical molecular configuration prior to admitting substantial identity. After all, a man does not lose his identity by an amputation or a major organ transplant. The principle of identity lies elsewhere. We find it in the form.

## Some Objections Answered

There are three objections which may be raised against our metaphysical anthropology:

1. We may be accused of arbitrarily buying into an ancient system of metaphysics. Let us break this criticism down into its various components.

a. Our resort to Aristotle is not arbitrary. It is a reasoned utilization of a metaphysics which we find most suitable to account for revelatory data. We indicated early on that this kind of suitability would be one of our criteria in selecting philosophical material. Resort to Aristotle would be arbitrary only if we were not willing to draw all necessary consequences out of our present use of Aristotle. Such would be the case if we resorted to Aristotle at this point and to some other metaphysics at another point, and the results were clearly contradictory; for example, if we somewhere accepted the nominalistic conclusion that there are no forms.

b. Did we buy into the Aristotelian system? In the light of the above assertions, have we committed ourselves to becoming Aristotelian on every point? It appears that this would be an overstated conclusion. Certainly we have committed ourselves to philosophizing in a certain direction. But the only necessity is for us to be consistent with this initial step we have taken in an Aristotelian direction, not to follow Aristotle on every subsequent point. As a matter of fact, Aristotle, at least as interpreted by Aquinas, will be viewed favorably on several occasions throughout the remainder of this book. But this is because his thought is applicable on those occasions, not because we have developed a blind loyalty to his system.

c. That the Aristotelian system is an ancient one ought certainly not to be an inherently telling feature against it. The age of a philosophical point is totally irrelevant to its truth or falsity.

But here the objection might go further. If we are trying to provide a philosophical framework from which the theologian can interpret revelation into the terms of his culture, is the recourse to Aristotle not a step backward in time? In answer to this, it should be noted that modernity in itself can never be a criterion for accepting a philosophical position. Although the philosophy should be applicable to modern man, priority has to be given to philosophical truth and coherence and to suitability for expressing revelation. Any system which does not have these priorities cannot be accepted, no matter how recent its origin.

In any event, we need not be too greatly concerned over this matter for in utilizing the Aristotelian position we are in fact not returning to a philosophical system which has lain dormant for the last 2,300 years. Aristotle has been revived and propagated over and over again, particularly by the writings and school of Thomas Aquinas, whose followers have not only persisted right into our century, but have continued to bring his system up-to-date. Thus at least a modified form of Aristotle's philosophy is a valid contemporary option. In fact, a number of twentieth-century thinkers find the Aristotelian conclusions to be true on their own merit apart from their theological applications. Although Aristotle's system may be "ancient," that does not mean it is "archaic." Of course, Aristotle's thoughts are not the thoughts of contemporary philosophers, such as Ludwig Wittgenstein and W. V. O. Quine.

But that does not make them any less current or applicable.

2. A second, more technical, objection is directed against the use of the Aristotelian notion of forms. This objection comes from two directions, the Platonic and the nominalist positions.

A Platonist may argue that he has received short shrift in our discussion. This is probably an accurate assessment. But let us remember that we dismissed Plato because of his theological unsuitability, not because of philosophical shortcomings. This is not to say that we have no philosophical objections against the Platonic notion of the independent reality of the Forms (as well as the anthropology which results therefrom) in contrast to Aristotle's notion of the unity of form and matter. It is just that in this context it is necessary for us to point out only that Platonism is inferior to Aristotelianism for the sake of prolegomena.[22]

A far more critical objection in the contemporary context will be raised by those who deny the reality of any such entity as a form altogether. Here we enter the ages-long nominalist-realist controversy which is still *mutatis mutandis* going on in this century. Our position is vulnerable to the nominalist attack.

In defense we note first that the persistence of this controversy gives us the encouragement that we are not making use of a position which has been definitively refuted. There is no danger, then, of obsoletism.

We note also that any nominalist critique which is premised on the impossibility of the existence of any reality other than material has already been put aside by us on presuppositionalist grounds and need not be dealt with here. This would be fertile ground for a discussion in philosophy of religion or apologetics, but not in prolegomena as we have defined it.

[22]Remarkably, critiques of Platonism begin with Plato's own *Parmenides* 126a–135d.

Although the Aristotelian realist position has not been
definitively refuted, we must nevertheless not be too op-
timistic about refuting the nominalist position. The whole
issue is tied in too closely with other metaphysical beliefs,
as Peter Strawson has recently argued.[23] It is neither possible nor wise to even attempt here a thoroughgoing pre-
sentation of the nominalist-realist controversy together
with a lengthy argument in favor of Aristotelian realism.
Once again let a summary suffice.

Realists in general maintain that there exist (or subsist,
to be more Aristotelian) realities which are not objects
themselves, but are what determine the nature of objects.
For example, the Aristotelian form specifies the substance.
Two substances are alike when they share similar forms.
We express this similarity by using the same word in naming the form. Thus we call both Jones and Smith "man,"
because they share the form of man. Nominalists counter
that there is no universal "man"; all that exists are individual men to whom we apply the same word, *man*—
there is no further reality behind the word. Extreme nominalism considers universals *flatus vocis*, that is, simply
the physical event of applying the same linguistic term
(a mere "breath of air") to various individuals.

But extreme nominalism does not work. Surely there
has to be some reason for applying the same linguistic
sounds to two individuals. It cannot possibly be a matter
of chance; there must be a reason for convention. Thus
most nominalists take a more moderate approach. They
will argue that it is illogical to posit an entity (such as a
form) behind an object. Rather we apply universal language on the basis of the concepts which we impose on
the world. Modern nominalists make reference to conceptual similarities, sets, family resemblance, or such artifi-

[23]Peter Strawson, "Universals," *Studies in Metaphysics*, Midwest Studies
in Philosophy, vol. 4 (Minneapolis: University of Minnesota, 1979), pp. 3–10.

cial devices as "language used *flatus vocis* with 'dot-quotes.'"[24]

What separates the moderate nominalist from the Aristotelian realist is a fine line. Like the nominalist the Aristotelian is not arguing for self-existing universals; the form exists only as the aspect of the substance as a whole which determines its specific nature. The Aristotelian does not even have any trouble conceding to the nominalist that there is a certain amount of arbitrariness involved in both the naming and recognition of various forms; people in different cultural or linguistic communities may very well disagree on what constitutes the forms of a set of objects. Yet such disagreements do not disprove the reality of the underlying subsisting forms. In fact it can be argued that these disagreements would not even occur if there were no underlying reality. Once the nominalist and the Aristotelian have come to agreement that there is something, no matter how minimal, within the object itself that determines its naming, the crucial gap between the two positions has been bridged.

Thus some form of minimal realism is inevitable. And this is all that the Aristotelian view calls for. Of course the debate can be carried on to a far deeper level than what we have argued here. The nominalist may even be justified to a certain extent if he joins the Platonist in accusing us of begging the question. But again, it is impossible to argue out all of the philosophical questions here. We have at least made a strong case for the plausibility of the Aristotelian realist position. And that is all that is required for our project.

3. Let us consider one final objection, not because it has a great amount of intrinsic force, but because it allows us

[24]Wilfrid Sellars, "Mental Events" (paper delivered at a symposium of the American Philosophical Association [Western Division] in Detroit, April 26, 1980). Cf. Richard E. Grandy, "Universals or Family Resemblances?" *Studies in Metaphysics*, Midwest Studies in Philosophy, vol. 4 (Minneapolis: University of Minnesota, 1979), pp. 11–17.

to make some important points in the course of our reply. This objection is that our view of man is unscientific. There is no scientific evidence that man is a unity composed of a form (the soul) and matter (the body). Although this observation is correct, it has no force as an objection. Can philosophical questions really be decided on scientific grounds? In times past such positivistic notions have had their share of adherents, but have always been notoriously self-defeating. Proof by the scientific method (in any of its various interpretations) is not a criterion for philosophical applicability.

It is at this point that philosophically-oriented theological anthropologies have recently attempted to endow themselves with a rather dubious scientific respectability. What comes to mind are schemes, such as the ones advocated by Pierre Teilhard de Chardin, Karl Rahner, and Paul Tillich,[25] in which the more spiritual side of man is seen as the culmination of the processes of biological evolution. In such a view man's spirituality—his soul and intellect—evolved along with man himself.

Because of the widespread acceptance of such views, several comments are in order. (a) Despite the attempt to synthesize theology with scientific developments, there is no place for such a scheme in modern evolutionary theory, which disavows all teleology and spiritual components. (b) Because of the difference in methodologies as well as the inherent tenuousness of the conclusions for any theory of cosmic evolution, it is not required that a philosophical anthropology accommodate itself to an evolutionary world-view. (c) An evolutionary vantage point is not ruled out by the foregoing items, but its necessity

[25]Pierre Teilhard de Chardin, *The Future of Man*, trans. Norman Denny (New York: Harper & Row, 1964); Karl Rahner, *Schriften zur Theologie* (Einsiedeln: Benziger, 1965), vol. 5, pp. 183–221, and *Foundations of Christian Faith*, trans. William V. Dych (New York: Seabury, 1978), pp. 26–35, 178–92; Paul Tillich, *Systematic Theology* (Chicago: University of Chicago, 1963), vol. 3, pp. 15–30.

is questioned. To go further and deny its plausibility requires criteria beyond the purview of this inquiry. It appears, however, that the slow emergence of man in the evolutionary scheme is extremely difficult to reconcile with the Genesis account of the special creation of man. Thus we favor a nonevolutionary view of man's creation. For the philosophical anthropology developed in this chapter, this question is moot; it cannot impugn our theory.

We have argued that a view of man which sees him as a unity of soul and body, reflecting the Aristotelian scheme of form and matter, is a felicitous way of coming to terms with biblical anthropology. The next chapter will explore man's spiritual side, particularly his capacity to receive and respond to divine revelation.

# 4

# Man

## *The Potential to Hear God*

We turn in this chapter to a question which is somewhat more theological in nature and, consequently, perhaps more open to philosophical groundwork. The question concerns the possibility within man to receive divine revelation. How can finite man experience infinite God?

This is a question which the Bible, being revelation itself, does not answer in the sense in which we are interested here. This is not unexpected; Scripture simply assumes that man can hear and respond to God's call and message.

Let us remind ourselves that by revelation we are referring to the more typical forms of revelation mentioned in the first chapter. There is general revelation, a knowledge of God from nature available to every man, and there is special revelation, the direct dealings of God with man in history (particularly in Jesus Christ) and their inscripturation. Only by implication will we make reference to such things as private visions and direct signs from God.

But, in any event, this chapter is not about the form of revelation; that topic will be dealt with in the next chapter. Our present concern is actually more basic: How is it that man can assimilate any form of revelation? What is it about man that allows him to respond to the infinite?

In a sense, these questions were answered already in the last chapter where we argued for an ontologically real spiritual aspect of man. Certainly the link between God and man will be found on man's spiritual side (though not exclusively so). But even though this observation refines the question somewhat, it does nothing to establish a link between God and man. It only recognizes man's spirituality; it does not account for his openness to pure Spirit, that is, God.

## Extrinsecism: God and Man as Aliens

In answering our questions, we will borrow an outline from the thought of Karl Rahner which distinguishes between extrinsecism and intrinsecism.[1] The first category we shall borrow from Rahner is extrinsecism. This is the view that our starting point has to be a gulf between God and man, expressed by the dichotomy of the natural and the supernatural. In this dichotomy man falls, of course, on the side of nature. But God's gracious revelation to man is not of this order. God's revelation is supernatural; it breaks in upon man from outside of him. Hence the name *extrinsecism* for this view.

This theory certainly has a lot going for it, including an apparent foundation in common sense. Does it not stand to reason that this is the most adequate depiction of the relationship between God and man? Surely God is totally separate from nature. Nature is finite, limited, and, yes, even sinful. God, on the other hand, is infinite and all-perfect. Hence, God's revelation must come to man totally from the outside. To attempt to locate God's revelation within man himself would appear to border on blasphemy. An illustration of this view can be seen in the early

---

[1] Karl Rahner, "Concerning the Relationship Between Nature and Grace," in *Theological Investigations*, trans. Cornelius Ernst (New York: Seabury, 1961), vol. 1, pp. 297–317.

writings of Karl Barth, frequently characterized as "dialectical" theology.[2] The dialectics consists in the essential opposition between man and God, nature and supernature. Barth himself describes this period of his thought as centering around the distinction between God and man.[3] The crucial point was "God's independence and particular character, not only in relation to the natural but also to the spiritual cosmos; God's absolutely unique existence, might, and initiative, above all in relation to man."[4] Barth goes on to recall, "What expressions we used . . . above all, the famous 'wholly other' breaking in upon us perpendicularly from above."[5]

Such a picture of God and man can allow for only one particular notion of revelation—a confrontation in which God speaks down to man.

Despite the advantages of extrinsecism it also carries problems. For one thing, extrinsecism makes an arbitrary assumption of what constitutes human "nature." One must a priori relegate to man's basic nature all those aspects which characterize him as finite, sinful, and alienated from God; and everything which draws him to God, the very capacity to hear God, is relegated to a place outside of nature in the supernatural. Thus the view that there is a gulf between man and God may not be entirely due to an inherently ontological distinction, but due to a presuppositional decision by the theologian.

Another problem is that the radical division between nature and supernature may in fact (and historically did) generate the exact opposite result from that intended by its advocates. Instead of giving man a minimal place in relation to God, extrinsecism may actually elevate him.

[2]This period of Barth's writing begins with the commentary, *The Epistle to the Romans*, 6th ed., trans. Edwyn C. Hoskyns (New York: Oxford University, 1968). The original was published in 1919.

[3]Karl Barth, *The Humanity of God*, trans. John Newton Thomas (Richmond: John Knox, 1960), pp. 38–46.

[4]Ibid., p. 41.

[5]Ibid., p. 42.

For such a theory endows man with a certain autonomy vis-à-vis God. After all, man already existed prior to the external advent of grace. Thus man may not have been doing well before revelation, but he was self-sufficient ontologically. It would always remain a possibility, then, for man to declare to God that he has no need of Him; he can always respond "no" to God's external revelation on existential grounds.

## Intrinsecism: God Known in Man

The logical opposite of extrinsecism is the idea that God is made known in man, not in the unique sense of the incarnation but in every man. Here we would say that God's revelation and man's reception are not externally opposed to each other, but are intrinsically related. God reveals Himself in and through man.

With such a theory the study of man becomes the study of God's revelation. Not that man is God or that God is less real, but that God is known within man. In other words, this position should not be confused with any philosophy akin to Ludwig Feuerbach's, where anthropology and theology are identical in the strictest sense.[6] Here we merely say that the site at which an objectively real God reveals Himself is within man.

An excellent example of intrinsecism is provided by the thought of Friedrich Schleiermacher. Schleiermacher argues in *On Religion: Speeches to Its Cultured Despisers* against those who have rejected religion on supposedly scholarly grounds. He charges them with not having paid sufficient attention to all of the ramifications of the nature of man. If they did, they would discover that a faculty of religious consciousness is part of humanity. One cannot

---

[6]Ludwig Feuerbach, *The Essence of Christianity*, trans. George Eliot (New York: Harper & Row, 1957).

come to terms with who man truly is without taking this religious facet into account.[7] The origin of this faculty is not in the realm of reason or morality, but in the category of feeling. There is a basic feeling which bears to man his religious affinities. In *The Christian Faith*, Schleiermacher describes this as a feeling of absolute dependence on God, or, "which is the same thing, [a feeling] of being in relation to God."[8] Thus from a consciousness of his own existence, man feels directed to something Absolute, something beyond himself. The logical sequence of this process, as Helmut Thielicke has rightly argued,[9] must be observed. It does not begin with a God who instills in man a feeling of absolute dependence, but it begins with man, who, on the basis of this feeling, works his way up to recognition of the independent existence of God. Thus for Schleiermacher, the source of revelation lies within man's subjectivity.[10]

That Schleiermacher regards this feeling as a genuine source of revelation, and not just as a feeling of divine inclination which must then be supplemented externally, is brought out by the fact that all of his subsequent systematic theology is an explication of the self-consciousness of the Christian community.[11] Scripture and theological dialogue do add a certain amount of objective knowledge to the basic feeling of dependence on God. But

[7]Friedrich Schleiermacher, *On Religion: Speeches to Its Cultured Despisers*, trans. John Oman (New York: Harper & Row, 1958), p. 16.

[8]Friedrich Schleiermacher, *The Christian Faith*, ed. H. R. MacIntosh and J. S. Stewart (Philadelphia: Fortress, 1928), p. 12.

[9]Specifically, Thielicke cautions us to understand Schleiermacher's scheme as a noetic method, not as a historical experience in the individual's life (*The Evangelical Faith*, trans. Geoffrey Bromiley [Grand Rapids: Eerdmans, 1974], vol. 1, pp. 43–45).

[10]At the same time, we must be careful not to exaggerate the subjectivism of Schleiermacher's thought. See Winfried Corduan, "Schleiermacher's Test for Truth: Dialogue in the Church," *Journal of the Evangelical Theological Society*, forthcoming.

[11]Schleiermacher, *Christian Faith*, pp. 26–31.

this feeling never ceases to be the ultimate source of revelation.

The inherently pious motivation for Schleiermacher's view provides its greatest strength. It attempts to do away with any concept of human nature which does not give credit to man's basic orientation toward God. Schleiermacher considers as inadequate any description of man apart from his religious capacity. This avoids one of the problems of extrinsecism: external opposition between man and God.

There is a difficulty with Schleiermacher's position, however. Having once entered the realm of human subjectivity, he cannot extricate himself from it. Although Schleiermacher never falls into the trap of believing that man can stand on his own two feet religiously, that is, that man is completely autonomous, it is difficult to see how one is to guard against slipping into a view akin to that of Feuerbach, who argued that God is nothing but a projection of human imagination. If ultimately it is the feeling which is the source of truth, the concept of God becomes nothing more than a hypothesis which may (albeit with great difficulty) be replaced. Theology may always give way to anthropology.

This criticism can be applied to all intrinsecist theories. They are inadequate because they turn revelation into self-revelation of man. In an Eastern religious context this would be perfectly acceptable (and here we may note Schleiermacher's own flirtation with Spinoza's pantheism); but for Christian theology, which maintains a strict ontological distinction between God and man, such a theory will not do.

## Speaker and Hearer

Having outlined two basic positions on the relationship of man to divine revelation, we seem to be faced with a dilemma. Extrinsecism posits a gulf between human nature and God which is bridged by revelation, but which leaves open the option of human autonomy apart from revelation. Intrinsecism begins with man as the fount of revelation and can also leave him there as autonomous. But surely this must be a false dilemma. There has to be a solution which will combine the best features of each view without their respective problems.

This solution must incorporate two crucial ideas:

1. God and man are ontologically distinct; in the process of revelation God addresses man in a mode which cannot be understood within the context of a philosophical system which takes only man into account.
2. Man, though ontologically distinct from God, is existentially inclined toward Him. Man has the capacity to receive God's revelation. This faculty is such an integral part of man that he cannot be rightly understood without it. Thus man is not autonomous.

A model which will incorporate these ideas is that of speaker and hearer. God is seen as speaking to man in revealing Himself. Man is the hearer of God's Word. Such a model is provided by Karl Rahner, for whom the capacity to hear God, the *potentia obedientialis*, is the distinguishing mark of man.[12] Since we have in this chapter already borrowed (and adapted) some of Rahner's concepts, let us for the moment pursue Rahner's ideas further.

Rahner argues that in every instance of knowledge by a human being, he makes reference to an entity under certain specifications. For example, one may know an object to be round, smooth, and hard. But such a judgment would not be possible if the intellect did not have an inherent capacity to scan, as it were, all the other descriptions under which the entity could have been known. For

[12]Karl Rahner, *Hearers of the Word* (New York: Seabury, 1969), pp. 67–68.

example, the object might have been flat or cubical, rough or lumpy, soft or liquid. Thus the intellect has at its disposal the sum total of conditions in which being manifests itself, and we have a reference to being-in-general in every instance of knowledge. But, Rahner finishes his argument, such a reference to being-in-general would not be possible if it were not grounded in Absolute Being, which is God.[13]

Thus Rahner argues that an integral part of all human knowledge is a grounding in the being of God. This grounding in the being of God, to which Rahner refers as the *Vorgriff*, establishes God as the ultimate reference point for all men, for all men know something. Thereby man stands in an implicit relationship to God. On the basis of this ultimate grounding, Rahner defines man in terms of an openness to God. For if knowledge is central to man's essence, and God is central to knowledge, then God is central to the essence of man. By this argument we have established an intrinsic potential in all men to hear God, the *potentia obedientialis*.[14]

But Rahner does not now fall prey to the fallacies of intrinsecism. Although the capacity to hear God in the sense described above is certainly an intrinsic one, Rahner, from a slightly different perspective, ascribes it to an experience of the grace of God. This is Rahner's notion of the "supernatural existential."[15] Man's capacity to be open to God cannot be part of his nature in itself except for God's grace already being at work. Rahner reverses the intrinsecist argument here. He begins with what we know to be due to God's grace. This he calls supernatural, that is, it is not part of human nature (considered by itself). Then he subtracts this supernatural from what we know about man in general, and the remainder constitutes hu-

[13]Karl Rahner, *Spirit in the World*, trans. William Dych (New York: Seabury, 1968), pp. 179–83.
[14]Rahner, *Hearers*, pp. 66–68.
[15]Rahner, "Nature and Grace," pp. 308–17.

man nature by itself. But of course this supernatural aspect is found in and describes all men, so it is an existential (i.e., a property of being) of man. Thus we have the supernatural existential in man, which makes communion with God possible, and avoids the problems of extrinsecism and intrinsecism.

Let us summarize what we have attempted to describe so far. We have outlined two alternatives (extrinsecism and intrinsecism) with regard to man's capability for receiving revelation. After pointing out some problems with both of those alternatives, we described a compromise model (i.e., speaker and hearer) which is intended to bypass those problems. We expounded in a little further detail Karl Rahner's view as an example of this model. Another example might be found in the thought of Paul Tillich, who, though in a slightly different setting, distinguishes three categories: heteronomy (man against God), autonomy (man by himself), and theonomy (God through man).[16] In any event, we have arrived at the pivotal conclusion that neither a cleavage nor an identification is a proper starting point for our understanding of the relationship between man and divine revelation. Man has an intrinsic capacity for receiving revelation, but revelation is God's independent Word.

## Implications of the Fall

What Augustine is said to have referred to as the "God-shaped vacuum" in every man should be fillable universally. In theory, every human being has the capacity to receive revelation. But the question arises whether access to this revelation may in fact be blocked to some extent in many men.

This question comes to us from theology and must in

[16]Paul Tillich, *Systematic Theology* (Chicago: University of Chicago, 1963), vol. 3, p. 250.

the last analysis be left in the hands of the theologians.
But in terms of our project we must take some philosophical account of the issue. The datum supplied by theology is that man is fallen and may not be at all attuned
to God's revelation. Theologians vary in the amount of
difficulty they see at this point, but most of them coming
from the evangelical traditions will say that, because of
man's fallenness, he cannot comprehend revelation without a prior work of restoration by the Holy Spirit.
It appears that Rahner treats this point far too lightly.[17]
If one believes that some men are fallen, one has to reckon
with the fact that not all men stand in an open relationship to God. And even though Rahner acknowledges the
theoretical possibility of there being those who deny their
supernatural existential, the universality of this existential (all existentials must be universal) makes such a
rejection a logical and practical impossibility. The implication of this is worked out quite consistently by Rahner
in his very broad universalism, centering on the "anony-
mous Christian."[18] In short, a universal potential must be
acknowledged, but we must also allow for the fact that it
may not always be actualized.

Analysis of man's capacity to receive revelation leads
into some very practical issues. For what we are referring
to is not some mystical intuition, an otherworldly canal
to man's soul, or even, pace George Fox, an "inner light."
Not denying the reality, or at least possibility, of such
concepts, we will merely leave them aside as inapplicable
to this study. For after all, we defined revelation in the
first chapter in terms of the concrete facts of Scripture.
The question then becomes: To what extent can man
understand and internalize these objective data as he is
presented with them? The capacity to receive revelation

---

[17]As pointed out in Winfried Corduan, "The Christology of Karl Rahner:
A Critique," *Journal of the Evangelical Theological Society*, forthcoming.

[18]Karl Rahner, *Schriften zur Theologie* (Einsiedeln: Benziger, 1954–    ),
vol. 5, pp. 136–59; vol. 7, pp. 187–213; vol. 10, pp. 531–47.

(the supernatural existential) in our framework thus consists largely in the intellect's capability of grasping some very definite pieces of information. Secondarily the will is enticed to respond to the data. The will is almost entirely in the domain of systematic theology, but we must make some reference to it in the course of this chapter's arguments (and in the final chapter, which deals with regeneration).

## Faith and Reason

The capacity to receive revelation is a faculty of the intellect. Insofar as revelation consists of the dissemination of information to man, its assimilation is merely a special case in the general area of epistemology. How can man recognize the propositions of revelation as true?

It is obvious that we are making certain assumptions concerning the nature of revelation. At this point, however, it is appropriate to be wary of reading too many assumptions into our statements. When we remark on the need to assent to the truth of revelatory propositions, that does not necessarily imply a linear propositional medium of revelation. All that needs to be granted here is that revelation conveys truth; and philosophically, not only can every truth be expressed propositionally, but propositions are the only means of predicating truth. Thus our idea of the necessity of assenting to revelatory propositions is neither unreasonable nor parochial. If revelation conveys truth, assent is inevitable.

Assent to propositional truth is the faculty of the intellect. The intellect has two modes of carrying out this task: faith and reason.[19] Right away it may be objected that faith is not a mode of the intellect at all; it is an expression

[19]For this assertion and much of the following discussion we are following very closely Thomas Aquinas, *Summa contra Gentiles*, trans. Anton C. Pegis (Garden City, NY: Doubleday, 1955), vol. 1, pp. 63–78.

of the will, or, metaphysically, the heart. We are dealing here with a basic equivocation on the word *faith*, which must be cleared away to make progress possible. Let us agree that "faith" can be used in two senses:

1. As Christians we hold that we are saved by faith. But it is not the faith itself which saves us, but faith *in* Jesus Christ. This kind of faith is certainly not intellectual; it is an exercise of the will toward the object of faith, the Savior. It is not this saving faith which we have in mind in this discussion. This faith presupposes knowledge of revelation. One cannot place one's faith *in* Jesus Christ until one believes *that* Jesus Christ is the Son of God, the Savior. "Faith *in*" is a completely theological category which has no further relevance to us at this point.

2. "Faith *that*" is the intellectual category to which we are referring. Here we mean an immediate assent to the truth of a proposition without any epistemological tests. As soon as a testing procedure is introduced, the faculty of reason becomes involved. Thus "faith *that*" means making a judgment of truth without rational grounds.

This is not to say that this faith is irrational in itself. "Irrationality" means that some canon of logic or proper thinking is violated, and this is certainly not the case. "Faith *that*" is not contrary to reason, but neither would it be accurate to say that it is rational, if by "rational" we mean that it passes the scrutiny of some test of reason. It is simply a-rational. A rational person can hold many propositions by faith without violating his rationality. "Faith *that*" is an important facet of human knowledge. We believe many things to be true on just that basis. Distinguishing between a source of truth and tests for truth, we can point out a large diversity of sources for beliefs: cultural assumptions, parental authority, other authorities, emotional inclinations, and so on. It may not be an overstatement in the least to say that no one's beliefs are completely based on rational grounds.

In religious matters, the acceptance of truth on the basis of faith is a clear option. The intellect may merely assent to whatever is presented to it by revelation. In fact, it is quite possible that the majority of people do receive their revelation this way exclusively, that is, by pure fideism. Thomas Aquinas argues that this is quite proper; after all, most men do not have sufficient opportunity, ability, or energy to undertake the rigors of an intellectual investigation of religious truth.[20] Thus fideism, as disreputable as its name may be, must be allowed as one valid avenue for knowing the truths of revelation.

However, a problem comes about if it is claimed that fideism is the only access to Christian truth. At this point serious debate must be carried out. Are there criteria for Christian truth which allow us to undertake rational tests?

We are not here going to distinguish between various epistemological methodologies. The question of whether we are talking about deductive rationalism, empiricism, or more complicated systems can be laid aside. For our purposes they are all "rational" in that the intellect passes judgment on the basis of whatever methodology is employed.

Now it appears that many of the beliefs which can be known by faith alone can also be tested and known rationally. Of course for any one person it can be only one way or the other: you cannot know something by faith alone and by reason. But two people can know the same item, one by faith and the other by reason. Items which could come under this heading include the existence of God, certain aspects of the nature of God, the veracity of Scripture, and other matters generally classed together as natural theology. But even when it comes to special revelation, one person may accept scriptural propositions by faith alone, whereas someone else may also want to understand and accept scriptural teachings on the basis of reason.

[20]Ibid., pp. 66–74.

In support of the claim that the same truth can be known by faith and by reason, we turn to a general ontology of truth. We believe that whatever is true corresponds to what is the case; and whatever is the case, expressed propositionally, is true. There are not two realms of truth: what is true, and what is really true. Either something is true or it is not.

Further, there is another exclusive disjunction: either reason conveys truth to us, or it does not. There is no halfway house between knowledge and skepticism. The often-used expression, "certain knowledge," is highly misleading if it tempts us to think that somehow there is such a thing as "doubtful knowledge." We are entitled to claim something is true if it meets our epistemological standards. Beyond that there are no standards for the standards, and we can confidently claim to know truth. The only alternative is skepticism. But of course the skeptics' claim is notoriously self-defeating. (Their attempt to suspend all judgment about reality is in itself a judgment about reality.) Therefore, we may conclude that rational criteria do reveal truth to us, and, thus, what is the case.

If the above conclusions are accurate—namely, that faith is a valid avenue for knowing truth, that there can be only one truth, and that reason (which may include any number of empirical or deductive methods) can reveal truth—the truth arrived at by faith and the truth arrived at by reason must be the same. A Christian can further bolster this argument by stating that, since God is Creator of the world in its totality, all truth must be derived from Him. Then those areas of truth to which reason may not have direct access (areas which can be known only by faith), such as the Trinity, may by the same token never be counterrational. Even though reason may not on its own discover these truths, it would be quite wrong to say that therefore they are contrary to reason, that is, contrary to logic.[21] There can be no double truth. If something is contrary to reason, it is false. Thus reason is also an acceptable tool for the assimilation of revelation. But now an argument against such use of reason comes to the fore. Is not reason too limited, particularly by the effects of the fall? It is difficult to see how such a stance can be maintained other than as an apodictic presupposition. But given such a presupposition, all rational arguments for the veracity of revelational claims are doomed from the start. This is certainly a rash decision in light of all the many arguments and tests for truth that can be adduced.

## The Validity of Reason

How valid is man's reason, especially when it comes to dealing with revealed matters? We begin with a very simple conditional argument.[22]

1. If there are no clouds, the sun is shining.
2. There are no clouds.
3. The sun is shining.

No rational person will reject the validity of this argument. Statement (3) follows clearly from (1) and (2).

---

[21]See the debate carried on in the *Journal of the Evangelical Theological Society*: John V. Dahms, "How Reliable Is Logic?" 21 (1978): 369–80; Norman L. Geisler, " 'Avoid . . . Contradictions' (I Timothy 6:20): A Reply to John Dahms," 22 (1979): 55–65; John V. Dahms, "A Trinitarian Epistemology Defended: A Rejoinder to Norman Geisler," 22 (1979): 133–48; "Avoid *All* Contradictions: A Surrejoinder to John Dahms," 22 (1979): 149–59.

[22]The idea of analyzing religious arguments by using absurdly simple paradigms is suggested by George I. Mavrodes, *Belief in God: A Study in the Epistemology of Religion* (New York: Random House, 1970), pp. 22–48. But for the sake of simplicity we are here ignoring Mavrodes's important distinction between proof and argument.

Only someone who is completely skeptical about the powers of reason would disallow this argument.

Now let us keep the same form of logic, but change the wording of the statements:

4. If there are no clouds, Christ is God.
5. There are no clouds.
6. Christ is God.

Again this is a valid conditional argument. Statement (6) follows from (4) and (5); the logic is impeccable. Yet few people would accept this as a successful argument for Christ's deity. But why would people not accept such an argument? The answer is that statement (4) is highly objectionable. Most of us would reject it. Consequently the argument fails. Although Christians accept (6) as true, they would not do so on the basis of (4) and (5).

Let us note why statement (4) is objectionable. It is because whether or not there are clouds on a given day is simply inadequate evidence for or against Christ's being God. It is not the operation of reason that is in question. The logic of the argument stands. It is the facts which go into the syllogism that constitute the barrier. If the facts were better, that is, if we had a more acceptable criterion than the weather, the argument would in fact hold.

The only way in which someone can at this point categorically dismiss the efficacy of any such argument is by an across-the-board denial of the existence of any evidence that could be correctly substituted for statement (4). This is a possible move, although it would be of dubious worth in light of the unity of all truth for which we argued earlier. But what cannot be done is to assault the operation of reason in our sample syllogism. We may question the content and adequacy of the evidence, but not the reasoning process. If we should, for the sake of argument, grant the truth of (4), we have in fact proven the deity of Christ.

The same holds true with regard to any truth conveyed by revelation and submitted to the reasoning process. There may be a question about the content and the adequacy of the evidence, but never about the legitimacy of the reasoning process.

It should be noted here that we are sidestepping the issue of the adequacy of the evidence if we begin to interpret all arguments in terms of probability. It makes no sense to (1) declare a deductive argument as invalid, but nonetheless showing probable truth; (2) declare a deductive argument as valid, but only in terms of probability; (3) declare a deductive argument as invalid, align it with a number of similar invalid arguments, and attribute probable truth to them on the basis of their cumulative force. What we are saying is that adequate evidence either exists or it does not. If it does, it shows (conclusively—for there is no other way) what it is intended to show. If adequate evidence does not exist, nothing whatever is shown. Probability can be used as a standard for evaluating the evidence, but not the validity of the reasoning.

We are making the point that reason per se can pass judgment on the truth and falsehood of matters which purport to be revelatory. It would be a sad state of affairs if it were otherwise. There would be no way of testing the credentials of any claim of revealed truth. Any statement could with equal justification (or rather, lack of justification) be passed off as true and to be believed. Surely, not many people would regard this as a desirable situation.

Moreover, rational people do in fact operate on the assumption that reason can pass judgment on the truth or falsehood of what purports to be revelatory. Even someone who rejects deductive or empirical criteria nonetheless probably uses a test for consistency within the Christian system (e.g., Karl Barth).

## The Noetic Effects of Sin

But what about the fall? We stated earlier that we must take into account man's fallenness and the effect this may have on his mind. It might seem that we have forgotten about this. But actually it is only now, after we have discussed the validity of reason in general, that it makes sense to describe the effects of the fall.

With certain qualifications, man's powers of reason are still intact. The qualifications are: (1) due to the fall man misuses his reason; and (2) until the created order is restored, there will be a limitation on the clarity with which man perceives the objects of knowledge. Let us address these two qualifications in order.

1. The Bible states that as a consequence of turning away from God, man's mental faculties became obscured (Rom. 1:21–22). This is linked directly to a rejection of the natural knowledge of God available to all human beings after the fall. Surely Paul is not writing here just about Adam and Eve; he is speaking in general terms of many people. Thus the disruption of reason is not attributed directly to the fall; rather it is an effect following from the perversion of man's will. Man's mind is darkened only after deliberately refusing to acknowledge God. Hence his fallen mind is due to the misdirection of his will. It is not so much that reason is not functioning properly, but that it is functioning apart from (and thereby against) its Creator.

The noted contemporary apologist, Cornelius Van Til, would undoubtedly not agree with our understanding of reason, but an analogy which he uses may be adapted to our view.[23] We may liken human reason to a saw which has never actually lost its sharpness. But it is set at the wrong angle. Consequently, no matter how well the saw cuts, it cuts wrong. The problem lies not with the saw,

[23]Cornelius Van Til, *The Defense of the Faith* (Philadelphia: Presbyterian & Reformed, 1955), p. 261.

but with the angle at which it has been set. So it is with human reason. The angle at which it has been set by the will is all wrong. But reason itself has not lost its sharpness. Recall for a moment our inane argument that Christ is God because there are no clouds. In this case reason is functioning clearly, but we have the wrong information. A mind turned against God will work with the wrong information and, consequently, the conclusion will be false.

Man's will needs to be restored (i.e., turned to God) before human reason can cut in the right direction. Theologians are carrying out their debates on what is necessary to bring this about, particularly how much prevenient work of the Holy Spirit is needed. We will not get into that issue here. We wish to emphasize only that nothing which contradicts plain reason can be true, and that nothing which reason shows to be true can be theologically false. The trick is to get man to use his reason in the direction of God.

2. In discussing the argument that Christ is God because there are no clouds, we noted that the problem lay with statement (4) in that it proposed weather conditions as evidence for the deity of Christ. This is clearly inadequate as evidence. But what if we changed (4) to:

4a. If Christ is raised from the dead, He is God; or
4b. If Christ is Savior, He is God; or
4c. If Christ returns, He is God,

would we not then have introduced matters which many people do consider evidence? Changing the content of the initial premise drastically increases the force of the syllogism which results from it.

Man's difficulty is that evidence such as that presented in the alternative premises is not as accessible as a mere consultation of the weather. Statement (4a) involves a historical judgment, (4b) a present theological affirmation, and (4c) a future expectation. They illustrate varying degrees of accessibility to data which can be used to construct a rational argument. Human reason, no matter how acute, is only as useful as the information with which it can work. To make further use of Van Til's analogy, the quality of cut a saw produces may be partially dependent on the type of material on which it is used. Here, in the assessment of the evidence, it may be of value for man to get into the issue of its probability.

The point of all this is that the quality of evidence is an important factor to consider. It will some day improve when regenerate man is changed into a glorified state. At present much of the evidence may be considered equivocal (though not necessarily all of it). When man has completely overcome the effects of the fall, that condition will be remedied. But it is the perceptibility of the evidence which will improve, not man's reason.

Such an understanding of man's future knowledge still allows us to maintain faith in the present reliability of reason. If we grant a future improvement in reason per se, this may mean either a lowered propensity to fall into rational errors or an increase in our consistency of applying rational principles. In neither case do we have to impugn present reason as long as we use it properly.

In this chapter we have shown that man has a capacity to hear God's revelation. This capacity is linked to the faculties of the intellect, which include valuable contributions from reason. Now we need to clarify this total picture by describing the nature of revelation as it comes to man.

# 5

# Revelation

## *The Historical Dimension*

The next step in our transcendental query after a philosophical grounding for theology must concern the nature of revelation as it addresses man. Given the nature of man, revelation must be such that it directly speaks to man. That is, in order for man to hear God, God must speak man's language. This chapter will explore how man can be universally addressed.

## Man as Historical Being

Man is a unit. In the last chapter we dealt at length with the nonmaterial side of man, but that should not be taken as meaning that from now on we can focus exclusively on this aspect. Let us remind ourselves once again that man is not an intellect imprisoned in a body, but a complete unity of body and mind. Thus man is not understood properly if his physical dimension is ignored.

Physical bodies are sometimes called "extended substances" (e.g., by Descartes). What this means in ordinary language is that bodies take up space, which is no profound insight. To compound the apparent inanity, let us also add the temporal dimension: bodies are localized on the time continuum; they come into being, persist, and pass away at certain points of time. For our present purposes it makes no difference whether we adopt the traditional paradigm of substances as bodies in space/time or the Whiteheadian metaphysics of substances as events. Nor do we need to quibble over how to conceive of time (cf. Kant's view of space and time as external and internal forms of consciousness respectively). The important point is that bodies must be considered within the space/time matrix.

These considerations also include human bodies, and here the inanity ends. Man, if considered correctly by including his physical aspect, must be seen within space and time. The universal, "man," is abstracted from the multitude of men, each of whom exists in a particular location and a definite segment of time. We will use existence in space and time as a minimal definition of the term *historical*. Under this definition every man is and can see himself as historical. The nonmaterial dimension comes into play in that man is conscious of his historical existence.

To go beyond our minimal definition of "historical," however, presents difficulties; for a large segment of the human population does not in fact share our concept of history, that is, the Judeo-Christian view. This brings to mind the outstanding work of the Romanian scholar, Mircea Eliade, and his analysis of primitive cultures.[1] In Eliade's view, primitive man has a unique concept of space and time, which clearly runs counter to our concept of history.

A primitive man's notion of space is directly tied in with a specific site which his particular culture or tradition in effect designates as the center of the world. This *axis mundi* may be a spear in the center of a village, a large tree, a Maypole, a church steeple, or the like. In

[1]Mircea Eliade, *The Sacred and the Profane*, trans. Willard R. Trask (New York: Harcourt, Brace and World, 1959); and *Cosmos and History: The Myth of the Eternal Return*, trans. Willard R. Trask (New York: Harper & Row, 1959).

nomadic cultures, as the tribe moves, so does the center of space. There is then no objective space in which events occur, but space is, as it were, invented by the people occupying it. In this understanding, space is really a culturally determined, yet arbitrary, convention.[2]

The conception of time is even more problematic. To the primitive, according to Eliade, time is cyclical. Every year is another revolution of a circle which continually repeats itself. Annual events reflect primitive mythology. For example, the gods' creation of the world is reflected in the annual springtime rejuvenation of the earth and the accompanying festivals. Similarly, the year is punctuated by other special occasions (e.g., community celebrations, personal commemorations, religious observances) which refer back to the days of old. Thus life consists of endless repetitions of the same cycle. There is no concept either of a beginning of history or of the flow of time toward a future. The annual cycle is always turning, and that is all there is to time.[3]

It is difficult to see how man in such a society could share our concept of history. The only notion he has of geographical space is one which he himself has created; and, even more crucial, he has no idea of a flow of history.

In contrast to the primitive's concept of time and space, let us look for a moment at the Western, Judeo-Christian understanding. Space is the expanse of the world as it was created by God. It is objectively real, whether it is filled or not. Time began at the point of creation and continues over all human generations until its consummation. The intervening history consists of an indefinite number of unique events which may be analogous as a class, but are nonrepeatable in themselves. History, then, is linear, with a definite beginning and a certain goal toward which it is progressing.

[2]Eliade, *Sacred*, pp. 20–65; *Cosmos*, pp. 8–17.
[3]Eliade, *Sacred*, pp. 68–113; *Cosmos*, pp. 51–92.

It may be apropos here to mention two other philosophies of history. Indian conceptions of time are spiral. In
Hindu thought, history consists of *kalpas*, cycles of time
lasting many millions of years. When each *kalpa* is finished, everything is destroyed by Shiva, Brahma creates
a new world, and, under the preserving care of Vishnu, a
new cycle starts. This process is repeated many times
over. Thus Hindu thought combines elements of the primitive cyclical view with a more history-conscious view.[4]
The modern secular view of history is a truncated version of the Judeo-Christian one. It retains the linearity,
but it removes both the beginning and the end of history.
History is merely an unending succession of events. One
can easily slip from this view back into a primitive cyclical
one, a danger which is also present whenever one
loses awareness of the historical grounding of the Judeo-
Christian tradition. Where there are no concrete bounds
to one's view of history, it becomes a meaningless sequence of pointless occasions. But people do in fact tie
their lives to some temporal boundaries and have some
sense of a cyclical history; otherwise annual and seasonal
events, for example, birthdays and holidays, would have
no meaning.

If we limited ourselves to the Judeo-Christian view of
history, then we would certainly not be justified in making
a general statement that man sees himself as "historical."
But we gave the word *historical* a far more encompassing
definition ("existence in space and time"). Under that definition, even primitive man sees himself as historical.

But we can go beyond our minimal definition if we
distinguish between man and his culture. Primitive culture certainly has no concept of history in the Judeo-
Christian sense. Primitive man has no concept of the events
of several generations ago. Things to him have always
been the way they are. But there is a sense in which the

[4]Eliade, *Cosmos*, pp. 112–18.

primitive individual does share our sense of history. He himself has a personal history; he has a past, a present, and a future, determined by birth, various rites of passage (which may include puberty and marriage), and death. He has done things in his lifetime. He can relate to other people and the events of their lifetimes, though such involvement may not be without a certain degree of difficulty, depending on the amount of cultural separation between them. Therefore it is possible to say that even primitive man has a historical orientation. Space/time is important to him; and if it is important to primitive man, it is all the more so to more "advanced" man.

So it is an important feature of man's existence that he is conscious of the flow of events through time and space and considers himself part of it. He is interested in what happened and his contributions to those events. In general he is concerned with what really took place; at least as it relates to his daily affairs he wants to know the difference between truth and fiction when reports are made to him. His life is tied into a nexus of historical occasions.

### Revelation as History

The next step in this transcendental argument is to show that revelation speaks to this historical orientation in man. In Christian theology, divine revelation is identified with the Bible; this concept seems to place revelation right into the realm of the propositional (see chapter 6). But the propositional presupposes the historical.

It has been said that at this point the uniqueness of the Judeo-Christian understanding is evident. In other religions the historical element takes a secondary place to the propositional teaching. For example, in Buddhism, it is the teaching of Siddhartha Gautama which is important; the events of his life are only examples of his teaching. The historical Buddha is irrelevant except as the source for his teachings. Once we cross from the more conservative traditions of Theravada Buddhism into Mahayana schools, where various Buddha figures and bodhisattvas are important, we find that we are no longer dealing with historical individuals.

In contrast, the Judeo-Christian tradition rides on history. The truth of the teachings is predicated on particular persons and events in history. The recorded form of the Mosaic law, for example, presupposes a historical Moses; and the teachings on the atoning death of Christ would be nonsense unless Jesus had really died on the cross in history.

Thus biblical revelation is historical revelation. Of course the Bible is not a uniform piece of writing; it is a collection of very diverse documents. Yet historicity is a factor in all of the components of the Bible.

1. *The Old Testament accounts of origins are historical.* The stories about the beginnings of the world and of the nation of Israel are both historical in nature. The style of these narratives is not poetical—the Hebrews had a clear way of writing poetry (parallelism) which is not used in these accounts. These stories are not didactic in the sense of merely conveying ideas, but record events which are clearly intended to be understood as having actually taken place in history (and were so understood by the Jews). There ought to be no big debate concerning the fact that at least as far as the original intent of these narratives, they describe a historical Adam, Noah, and Abraham.

It is at this point that we must discuss the important category of myth. Most critics of the historicity of the biblical accounts of origins would place them into the realm of the mythical. No claim would then need to be made for the historical facticity of the accounts. For myths are not intended to convey historical truth, but to serve as explanatory vehicles. Therefore we could recognize these stories as serving to give faithful accounts of the beginnings of what was important to the Hebrews, but would not construe them as somehow objectively describing actual events.

A myth is a story giving a narrative account of a central truth in terms most relevant to the culture in which it arises. Thus the actual content of the myth is dispensable as long as the central truth is preserved. For example, it might be said that the story of the creation is a mythological way of saying that everything which exists is due to God. We could express this same truth in a different myth or in a demythologized form. Whatever we do, it is clear that no value ought to be attached to the narrative components.

In commenting on the subject of myth, we must be careful not to go too far. Certainly myths exist exactly in the terms described. Not every story of origins in the world is, or could be, true. If along with rehabilitating the historicity of Adam and Eve we also establish Izanagi and Izanami (of the Japanese Kojiki), we have clearly gone overboard. On the other hand, there may not be anything wrong with describing the biblical accounts as "myths" if we want to emphasize their etiological character. The question is whether that label would automatically impeach the historical veracity of the facts they relate.

In addressing this question, we must take cognizance of a particular philosophical prejudice. The assumption that the loftiness of spiritual truth demands that it be freed from the mundaneness of the contingent facts of history is the legacy of particularly influential persons in the history of philosophy (e.g., Plato and G. W. F. Hegel).[5] How can finite facts ever convey eternal truths? One who holds this presupposition will tend to see biblical accounts as mythical representations of spiritual insights rather than as mere historical occurrences.

Two points can be made in reply: (a) Any epistemology

[5]Cf. Norman Geisler, ed., *Biblical Errancy: An Analysis of Its Philosophical Roots* (Grand Rapids: Zondervan, 1981).

which feels free to dispense with concrete facts can lead
only to subjectivism, along with its blood relation, skepticism. If the facts are irrelevant, nothing relevant can be
said. (b) The view that spiritual truth should be free from
historical facts would be appropriate to a certain extent
if the Platonic view of man were correct, that is, if the
spiritual side of man were the only important one, and
man were not existentially historical. But we have shown
that the Platonic view is inadequate. Man, as a concrete,
historical being with a physical side as well as a spiritual
side, needs to be spoken to in a concrete, historical, and
physical way. This is accomplished only if history is allowed to stand without being sublimated into the nebu-
lous realm of myth.

It must be observed that if the label *myth* precludes
historical facticity, it will not apply to the stories of origins
in Scripture. If facticity should be allowed, then nothing
is gained by the label; for if myth is intended to point up
the author's explanatory intent, the stories are in no different category from other historical writing. There is no
such thing as purely objective, detached historiography.

Now the problem of whether the accounts in question
are actually true cannot be treated here adequately. That
comes under the heading of apologetics, which we have
distinguished from prolegomena. Suffice it to say here
that on the basis of many apologetic efforts, one can confidently accept the truth of those passages without com-
mitting intellectual suicide. An orthodox theologian of the
persuasion we have chosen as our paradigm, ought certainly to do so.

But all of this is somewhat off the main point. The
accounts definitely purport to tell historical truth. To re-
peat an earlier argument, the only genuine choice is to
accept them that way or to reject them.

2. *The Bible contains many historical accounts.* In sur-
veying the various passages of Scripture, it becomes apparent that much of what it contains is historical writing

in the contemporary sense of the term. It needs to be given the same amount of credibility that is usually accorded historical documents.

A hundred years ago such a statement would have been subject to far more challenge than it is today. Modern archaeology has clearly again and again vindicated the historicity of Scripture. It is hard to imagine that once the Bible was lampooned for containing references to Ur of the Chaldees, which, everyone was quite sure, was utterly fictional. Now Ur's remains have been excavated and it is known to have been a significant power in its day. Similarly, archaeology has consistently confirmed the truth of all biblical matters it has touched on; not one biblical claim has been shown to be false by archaeological scrutiny.

Again, however, the issue of truthfulness is not of central concern here. It is most properly treated in apologetics. What we wish to emphasize is that the Bible contains a large amount of material which meets normal standards for historical writing.

We include among the historical passages the four Gospels and the Book of Acts. The Gospels, in particular, have been attacked as being unhistorical. They were written by people, it is claimed, who were so much under the spell of their experience with Jesus Christ that their accounts are expressions of their faith, not accurate historical narratives. We must discount the historicity of the Gospels on the basis of the all-too-evident subjectivity of their authors.

Such an attitude can be attributed to one of two causes: (a) a presupposition that a completely unprejudiced writing of history is possible—a patent absurdity; or (b) a predisposition against the Gospels on the basis of their supernatural character. The latter can be remedied only by a correct theistic world-view, not by historical argument. So, we will regard the Gospels as historical writings which are on a par with any other historical documents.

Thus we are confronting a historical Christ along with the historical acts of God.

3. *The teaching portions of the Bible are highly historical.* If we had to categorize the Bible as either textbook writing or historical writing, it would definitely be placed in the latter group. Let us (perhaps rather arbitrarily) define a textbook as a book in which certain facts are laid out as true without much regard for the immediate historical surroundings. For example, this present work is only minimally influenced by current political and social conditions. A more historical book, on the other hand, would make direct reference to, and be heavily influenced by, all kinds of surrounding factors.

The Bible, even in its didactic sections, falls into the category of historical. Whether we are talking about the Prophets, the Epistles, or other passages, the teaching is always understood better when historical circumstances are taken into account; and frequently they cannot be understood at all apart from their historical *Sitz im Leben.* Historical awareness is a precondition for thorough theological awareness.

Some might see the Bible's historical character as a genuine drawback. Would it not be far more advantageous to man if the historical element were eliminated (or eliminable), and we had something more like a spiritual textbook in which all that we are to believe is set out categorically? There would be no disputes about difficult passages, no problems with sections whose meaning might be lost to us. Everything would be clearly and unequivocally set out for universal acceptance.

The problem with this idea is that it would actually be counterproductive. As a matter of fact, it would be an extremely parochial form of revelation. Since all language is dependent on culture, such a spiritual textbook would speak clearly to one culture, but not to others. The further removed from the original culture, the more obscure it would be. Cultures which are very different would be totally excluded from revelation. There would be no common denominator to allow for access to revelation.

A historical revelation, on the other hand, can speak universally because it directs itself to the historical orientation of every man. There are difficulties, to be sure; but, since every man can relate to historical experience to some extent, there is no problem with skepticism.[6]

Thus the Bible, even in its teaching passages, is thoroughly grounded in historicity. What we have said here about didactic passages also applies, *mutatis mutandis*, to poetic and apocalyptic portions of Scripture. They are also thoroughly historical in content and outlook.

Our conclusion is, then, that man's historical character is addressed directly by a divine revelation cast in the form of historical writing. This conclusion, however, compels us to examine a difficult question only lightly touched upon so far.

## Making Sense of History

Can we make sense of history? We have to turn to the issue of a philosophy of history because it can very easily be claimed that history cannot be known, that all we have are probable conjectures or subjective interpolations, neither of which can yield genuine knowledge. This claim arises in two different approaches to history: (1) the positivistic and (2) the metaphysical.

1. It must be remembered that the historian does not study the events of history themselves. In a manner analogous to the work of a scientist, he consults the evidence, from which he builds his theories and hypotheses. In the study of history, this evidence takes the form of written

---

[6]Although Karl Rahner is not as concerned with the localization of revelatory propositions in Scripture, he does argue for a space/time concept of history as the foundation of man's receptivity to revelation. See *Hearers of the Word* (New York: Seabury, 1969), pp. 150–63.

documents and (to a limited extent) oral reports. The historian analyzes these documents, and from this evidence
pieces together the historical narrative to the best of his
ability. So far there is not much question of historiographical
procedure. But now the positivist points us to the fact
that the historian is not merely collecting documentary
evidence. He sorts out the best evidence, he infers causal
relationships between events, and he makes value judgments on the events. The results of all these activities are
the contribution of the historian; they are not explicitly
given within the documents themselves. Or, to put it differently, the historian interprets history; history does not
interpret itself.

But then the historian has to make a difficult choice.
He can acknowledge that all of his reports are the result
of his bias and forego any claim to scientific rigor. Or he
can accede to demands for scientific rigor and limit his
historical observations to generalizations which have status only as probable correlations. In either case it becomes clear that we can gain no certain information from
history and must content ourselves with guesswork which,
of course, may lead to skepticism.[7]

2. The metaphysical approach to history begins with
presuppositions which are clearly set out. It sees history
from the vantage point provided by a certain metaphysical perspective. The most famous example is in the writings of G. W. F. Hegel, for whom history constituted
the concrete self-unfolding of Spirit.[8] But we can also include any other description of history which begins with

[7]A very moderate form of a positivistic view of history is presented by
A. J. Ayer, *The Problem of Knowledge* (Baltimore: Penguin, 1956), pp. 153–64.
Cf. Arthur F. Holmes, *Faith Seeks Understanding* (Grand Rapids: Eerdmans,
1971), pp. 63–69.

[8]G. W. F. Hegel, *The Philosophy of History* (Magnolia, MA: Peter Smith,
n.d.).

an idea of what history should or must be like, and then uses the documentary evidence to corroborate this view. The problems with this approach are evident. Two thinkers coming from different metaphysical backgrounds will have two different theories. The result has to be subjectivism, again leading to skepticism. Thus both a positivistic and a metaphysical approach to history can lead to skepticism. Is there any way to escape this dilemma? If we cannot find one, historical revelation will be a useless idea. Under those circumstances, we might be able to gain some empathy with previous generations, in line with the subjective hermeneutic of Wilhelm Dilthey,[9] but history could not carry any objective authoritativeness.

But surely the problem is overstated. Skepticism need not be the immediate consequence of inquiry into historical methodology. Let us begin by making some emendations to the positivistic view.

First, some historical facts can be questioned only on the presupposition of skepticism. For example, there can be no reasonable doubt that Napoleon, the emperor of France, was defeated at Waterloo. An analysis of the reasons for Napoleon's defeat might be subjective, but not the occurrence of the event itself. Still, even in the subjective analysis, the historian should be guided by the available evidence; the best historian is the one who comes to terms with the evidence most thoroughly.

Second, there are criteria for judging historical evidence. Judgments need not be entirely subjective. The historian will generally resort to such standards as (a) whether there are multiple sources attesting to an event; (b) whether a source has a general reputation for truthfulness and reliability; (c) whether a source originated at about the time of the event described or later; (d) whether

[9]Wilhelm Dilthey, *Pattern and Meaning in History*, ed. H. P. Rickman (New York: Harper & Row, 1961).

circumstances encouraged truthfulness in a source. The list could go on, but is sufficient to point out that historians are guided by generally accepted criteria. This does not rule out subjective bias and metaphysical assumptions entirely. But we can mitigate that factor as well. Metaphysical conceptions are not necessarily arbitrary presuppositions, for there are philosophical methods for testing metaphysical systems. One of these is correspondence with the empirical world, in which we can include the events of history. Alfred North Whitehead's analogy of metaphysics as an airplane which must occasionally land to refuel seems applicable here.[10] Metaphysics need not be independent of facts. It may be judged and determined by facts.

Thus we are arguing for a view of history similar to what Arthur Holmes has called "interpretative realism."[11] There can be no question that a thorough study of history demands the interpretative work of the historian. But such a concession need not lead to skepticism. In fact, the opposite is true: There would be no point to historical research and testing were there no bedrock of historical facts which can indeed be known.

Let us summarize then. Man is a historical being who is addressed by a historical revelation. And the epistemological criteria of historical knowledge do not prevent us from regarding this revelation as true knowledge.

[10]Alfred North Whitehead, *Process and Reality* (New York: Free Press, 1979), p. 5.
[11]Holmes, *Faith*, p. 78.

# 6

# Revelation

## *The Propositional Dimension*

In the last chapter we showed that the historical nature of revelation speaks to the historical essence of man. This historical content comes to man in the form of propositions, thereby also including man's intellectual side. In this chapter we shall explore this propositional dimension of revelation and several implications arising out of it.

### A Propositional Account of History

In our discussion of historical methodology we listed some criteria for judging the reliability of historical sources (p. 93). Careful scrutiny will reveal that biblical history meets these criteria: (a) The Bible contains multiple accounts of the same event from different perspectives (e.g., the four Gospels) and is also corroborated by external historical documents. (b) Archaeology has consistently endorsed the reliability of the Bible. (c) Biblical sources contain eyewitness and first-hand accounts (at least that is their claim). (d) The biblical authors, firmly committed to the Decalogue, had high ethical standards which would go a long way toward preventing prevarication. Thus they were motivated not to falsify the historical records for the sake of personal or national aggrandizement. Other ancient writers tend towards self-glorification, oftentimes at

the expense of the facts; the Hebrew records are notable
for their brutal honesty with regard to both the flaws and
achievements of the nation and its rulers. And the New
Testament writers would not even have received a hearing
had they been guilty of historical falsehoods. Thus the
biblical authors were motivated by a need and desire for
truth.

All of the foregoing can serve as a basis for appropri-
ating Scripture as genuine history with a bona fide claim
to truth. We have here historical records which intend to
convey truth to us. Hence we must take the biblical propositions and come to terms with the historical message
they bring.

Now propositions do not exist as objective entities in
themselves. They are part of the process of communication. There are a speaker and a hearer, and the proposition
has value only insofar as it produces an interaction between the two. This requires intent, meaning, and understanding, which are not components over and above the
proposition, but are integral aspects of this whole communication process within what Ludwig Wittgenstein
called a "language game."[1]

Thus there is a context of communication within which
the historical propositions of the Bible appear. The biblical scholar, pursuing his exegesis, must keep this in mind;
proper understanding can be had only as he is conscious
of the cultural environment which produced the biblical
documents. That this can never be realized 100 percent
is obvious. Nonetheless, it is only through understanding
the original cultural environment that any proper assimilation can be obtained. Even the lay person goes through
this process, for he does have an awareness of the most
elementary differences between his world and the biblical
world.

[1]Ludwig Wittgenstein, *Philosophical Investigations*, trans. G. E. M. An-
scombe (New York: Macmillan, 1953), pp. 60–61, 168–72.

For our purposes, the point is that, when we assert the truth of revelational propositions, we do so with the qualification that (as with any other propositions) awareness of their truth is dependent on historical-grammatical exegesis. This qualification does not beg the question, but it merely applies what is true for any language event to this particular case.

Our claim that the propositional revelation of Scripture is truthful, or, to put it negatively, inerrant, has to be seen as all-encompassing. As we have shown, the propositional truth rides on historical reality. The spiritual, theological, and ethical aspects of the Bible arise out of the historical, geographical, and scientific facts. Thus no dichotomy between, say, the historical truths and the spiritual truths is possible; the historical cannot be rejected and the spiritual nonetheless affirmed. If the historical goes, so does the spiritual. We have already argued that that kind of historical dependency gives revelation its character of particular suitability for man.

Objections to this view of revelational truth are plentiful, but few are philosophically relevant. A great number of them arise from the perception of errors or inconsistencies in Scripture. Accepting the logical criterion that all it takes is one error to disprove biblical inerrancy, the scholar who is committed to biblical truth needs to account for those points which are in question. Such work is being carried on extensively in the field of apologetics and biblical scholarship—with at least sufficient success to lend intellectual respectability to the theory of inerrancy.

There are theological objections to inerrancy. They generally take the approach that human sinfulness demands that the Bible, written by humans, must contain flaws. John Gerstner has called this the "docetic non sequitur," after the notion that, if humanity always implies error, Jesus Christ must have been either not human (Docetism) or not perfect.[2] In any event, this objection has its roots in a Platonic philosophical presupposition which exalts truth of the spirit over truth of fact. We have already argued that this constitutes a misunderstanding of man and a flawed epistemology. There are no direct philosophical objections to complete scriptural truthfulness. How can there be a basic principle that makes it impossible for a book to contain nothing but true proposition? A simple illustration might be useful here.

No sensible person would deny that it is possible to write or utter a true proposition (by any standard of truth). For example:

1. It has rained today.

A second true proposition can be added:

2. My lunch today consisted of macaroni and cheese.

This simple accumulation of true propositions does not mean that all of a sudden one of them has to be false. If I can add another true proposition, there is no reason why I cannot add another hundred thousand. No philosophical argument can show a priori that a book full of propositions cannot be completely truthful.

Certainly the probability of errors increases as fallible humans write or talk with increasing frequency. But acknowledging that fact is far from asserting the impossibility of avoiding error. Theologically this is handled by the doctrine of inspiration with its corollary that the Holy Spirit kept the biblical authors from error. Philosophically, no such help is necessary to assume the possibility of inerrancy.

[2]John H. Gerstner, "The View of the Bible Held by the Church: Calvin and Westminster Divines," in *Inerrancy*, ed. Norman L. Geisler (Grand Rapids: Zondervan, 1980), p. 389.

## Revelation and Language

A far more interesting philosophical question arises at this point. This is the issue of whether language is in fact capable of conveying divine revelation. Granted that language can give us historical information, we are still a long shot away from information about the divine realm. And with regard to language about the divine, there are special problems.

There are two basic modes of language. In the univocal mode, a word is used with the same meaning throughout different contexts. In the equivocal mode, the same word takes on two or more different meanings. For example, the word *card* may refer univocally to both the identification one may carry and the ace of spades. But when Smith, who likes to engage in jokes and pranks, is called a "card" by his friends, they do not literally mean that he is a flat rectangular object. They are using the word equivocally.

Historical discourse is univocal. In fact, the recounting of history would make no sense if we did not take the terms of the narrative and relate them as univocally as possible to terms of our own experience. If we did not know precisely what is meant by "king," "battle," "reform," and other words typical of historical writing, there would be no point in attempting to come up with a plausible historical account. Hence, insofar as revelation is historical, there is no problem with the language; it is univocal.

But of course in the process of the historical narrative, we catch the divine narrative as well. Ultimately, we are being given information about God. Now the problem becomes real. When we talk about God, the danger of equivocity arises. To understand this, we must look at the nature of language for a moment.

There are two basic schools of thought today on the

acquisition of language.[3] One side holds that all language structure is acquired concomitantly with a child's learning to speak; the other view is that every human being has an innate language structure which gives him the capability to assimilate language into basic patterns. But the controversy surrounds only the structure of language, particularly grammatical functions; neither side would deny that actual language content is learned by the child in his developmental years. The words are not there already only to be slowly unveiled à la Platonic recollection. They still must be acquired.

The acquisition of actual language is a slow and complicated process based on a person's gradually becoming acquainted with his world, the people in it, and the requirements for survival in it. A child must learn to use particular sounds in a way which produces an intended result in communication, whether that consists of naming an object correctly or getting someone to meet a specific need. Through a gradual process of success and failure, the child becomes a communicating member of his society.

Every person acquires language within his own immediate personal and cultural environment. Language is, then, extremely changeable, for it will change as the environment changes. Language is always slightly imperfect, as ever new challenges in the form of new situations present themselves to a linguistic society. What we want to emphasize here above all is how much our human language is tied to this finite world.

But when we enter the realm of revelation, we are using this finite language to talk about infinite realities. We are making language refer to objects and experiences which are beyond our receptive capabilities. Specifically, when we speak of God and His nature, we know that we are

[3]See Noam Chomsky, *Current Issues in Linguistic Theory* (Hawthorne, NY: Mouton, 1964); and Milka Ivic, *Trends in Linguistics*, trans. Muriel Heppell (Hawthorne, NY: Mouton, 1965), esp. pp. 203–08, which deal with Chomsky's generative semantics.

referring to one who is all-perfect; hence our linguistic categories apparently cannot apply. For example, God's love is far greater than any human love; His justice exceeds our understanding of justice; and His sovereignty is an idea which goes beyond our concepts. Therefore, it appears that we are using language equivocally when we talk of God. This would seem to imply that we really do not know what the words mean, and, consequently, we are once again confronted by that old bogey, skepticism. We cannot then talk meaningfully of a propositional divine revelation.

However, let us remember the transcendental approach we are taking in this study. On the assumptions we laid down in the first chapter, we do accept propositional revelation and the fact that our God-talk is meaningful. So we need to ask a transcendental question: How is it that we can apply to an infinite God language derived from our finite environment? In other words, the question is not whether we can talk about God, but how it is possible that we can talk about Him.

## Mechanism for Religious Language

Even if this were a different kind of work, say a survey of philosophy of religion, it would not be possible to present all of the various theories that have been proposed concerning religious language. But we should have at least a general awareness of the options. So we will attempt to outline some of the theories that have been suggested.

### Religious Language as Self-determinative

Our discussion of the acquisition of language could be carried further. It could be said that all language is learned from its use, and the use of words is determined by the community. If someone enters a religious community, he will learn religious language in order to succeed in living within that group. That language will be a self-sufficient vehicle for communication; that is, there will be no need for criteria outside of this community to determine the meaning of words. In Wittgenstein's phrase, this setting constitutes one particular "language game" which is autonomous of all other language games.[4] Under this theory, God-talk is liberated from the need for a univocal relationship with language used elsewhere. The requirement for anyone wishing to learn the meaning of religious language is to place himself in the context where such language is used. No outsider can use the language properly or pass judgment on its sense. If there are rules governing the correct or incorrect use of religious terms, they will be provided by the language game itself. Thus religious language rules sovereignly over its own domain without any external interference. This view of religious language is held with various modifications by some followers of Wittgenstein (e.g., R. M. Hare[5] and Frederick Ferré[6]), and to some extent by the negative critics associated with logical positivism,[7] for whom the religious language game is on a par with other metaphysical utterances, even though it is only emotive.

It does not take much to see that this type of theory is nothing more than an attempt to endow equivocity with respectability. Nothing is actually accomplished with regard to the original problem. To our question as to how it is that religious language can be meaningful, the only answer here is that it simply is meaningful. That is not very satisfactory. An outsider confronted with religious propositions (perhaps directly from revelation) needs to be able to judge whether they are meaningful or not. Yet, according to this theory, how would he able to accord

---

[4]Wittgenstein, *Investigations*, p. 5.

[5]R. M. Hare's contribution to the symposium, "Theology and Falsification," in *New Essays in Philosophical Theology*, ed. Antony Flew and Alasdair MacIntyre (London: SCM, 1955), pp. 99–103.

[6]Frederick Ferré, *Language, Logic, and God* (New York: Harper & Row, 1961), pp. 155–59.

[7]A. J. Ayer, *Language, Truth, and Logic* (New York: Dover, 1946), pp. 114–20.

them assent, other than to have joined the religious community in the first place?

Nor does this theory appear to be suitable from the point of view of the religious insider. As Antony Flew (himself an "outsider") has argued quite rightly, part of the nature of religious language for the believer is that it is cognitive in a sense which places it on a par with other forms of language.[8] When the Christian says that God loves the world, he thinks of himself as in fact making a cosmological assertion, imparting certain truth which ought to be subject to normal criteria of meaning. The intent of religious language goes beyond talking to oneself in semiprivate utterances. The theory that religious language is self-determinative does not satisfactorily account for this intent.

*Univocity*

Just as the previous theory is an attempt to make equivocity respectable, it is also theoretically possible to subscribe to the opposite theory—univocity. The argument runs as follows:

1. There are only two types of language options: univocity and equivocity.
2. If religious language is equivocal, it cannot be used meaningfully.
3. Religious language is used meaningfully.
4. Therefore, it is not equivocal.
5. Therefore, religious language is univocal.

Unfortunately such an attempt at reasoning away the problem does nothing to solve it. The question as to *how* it is possible for religious language to be genuinely meaningful remains totally unanswered.

[8]Antony Flew in "Theology and Falsification," pp. 107–08.

*Meaning from Above: Catalogy*

We must again face the fact that, difficulties or no, the religious propositions that constitute revelation are thought of as meaningful. If we find it problematic to account for this phenomenon on the basis we have laid out, perhaps the reason is that we have chosen the wrong basis. Maybe we are approaching our subject matter backwards. Instead of starting with human language in general and then applying it to revelation, we might do better by taking revealed language as our starting point.

An approach of this type is taken by Karl Barth, to cite just one example.[9] In discussing the starting point of prolegomena we already indicated that Barth, eschewing all forms of natural theology, locates the origin of all theology in God's self-revelation in Jesus Christ (p. 31). Further, for Barth revelation comes to man from the outside with no basis intrinsic to man. It follows that on this point, too, Barth takes a totally theocentric viewpoint. A discussion on religious language can be meaningful for Barth only on the presupposition that God spoke first of all, and it is His speech which provides the standard for all other speech.[10]

In his later writings Barth admits a certain kind of analogy (see the following section) which attempts to bridge the gap between God (and revelation) and man (and human language). But this analogy is located first of all in the God-man, Jesus Christ. God in Christ provided an archetype of which the rest of creation is a copy.[11] This

[9]Karl Barth, *Church Dogmatics*, II. 1, trans. T. H. L. Parker et al. (Edinburgh: T. & T. Clark, 1957), pp. 228–43.

[10]"It is to be noted that the human word receives concrete content and concrete form from God, and becomes capable of saying something by the fact, and only by the fact, that it is spoken on the strength of God's permission and command, and therefore has the definite similarity with its object which is promised and bestowed by God's revelation, and is not arbitrarily discovered and affirmed" (Ibid., p. 232).

[11]Barth, *Church Dogmatics*, I. 2, trans. G. T. Thomson and Harold Knight, p. 10.

form of analogy thus begins from above with God and is then applied to man. Perhaps it is better called a *catalogy* rather than *analogy*. Forms of catalogy are also held by Gordon Clark[12] and Carl F. H. Henry,[13] to mention just two more examples. In all instances, catalogy holds that revelational language is the standard for all language.

There are two problems with catalogy: (1) It takes insufficient cognizance of the fact that revelation is this-worldly, concrete, and historical. Revelation does not consist in God's speaking to us in His language, but in our language. And this is exactly the problem, that it is our time-bound finite language which must serve as the vehicle for disclosure of the infinite. Catalogy is still saddled with the problem that finite language is all we have. To arbitrarily decree that revelation provides the linguistic standard does not solve anything. (2) Catalogy does not reckon with the way in which human language is acquired. As we argued earlier, we learn language from our immediate environment. It is not until after we know language that we are exposed to the text of revelation. No one learns a language by listening to recitations from the Bible. Hence, like it or not, general language is the starting point and religious language the special case. Catalogy constitutes a backward approach, and, possibly, a mere begging of the question.

*Analogy*

The majority of writers on the topic of religious language propose some solution which would in general terms

---

[12]Gordon H. Clark, *Religion, Reason and Revelation* (Nutley, NJ: Presbyterian & Reformed, 1961), pp. 142–46. Clark actually argues in terms of an innate language which is supplied to man by God and is thus the paradigm language. It is most clearly exemplified in the Bible and the Westminster Confessions.

[13]Carl F. H. Henry, *Notes on the Doctrine of God* (Boston: Wilde, 1948), p. 145. We should also mention Cornelius Van Til, *The Defense of the Faith* (Philadelphia: Presbyterian & Reformed, 1955), p. 39.

come under the heading of analogy. Analogy seeks to bridge the gap between univocity and equivocity. But this is not easy; in fact, it may be impossible.

Let us, for the sake of argument, imagine a spectrum of gradations between the univocal and the equivocal. Towards the univocal side there would be decreasing equivocity; in the other direction, univocity would be diminished.

```
                    decreasingly equivocal
                ◄──────────────────────────
univocity       ──────────────────────────►       equivocity
                    decreasingly univocal
```

Now let us imagine a point about midway on that continuum. It seems as though we then have a happy medium combining equal doses of univocity and equivocity. We could call this midpoint analogy.

The problem is that a halfway point between univocity and equivocity is still equivocity. It does not matter how small the equivocal element is; if a word is used in more than one way, be the difference ever so slight, the result is still equivocity. Thus the diagram should actually look like this:

```
univocity [◄──────────────────────────── equivocity
```

Everything to the right of the bracket is equivocal. The slightest departure from univocity is equivocity. Various proposals of analogy (under different names) as a means of understanding religious language founder on precisely this point. Let us look at three examples.

1. I. M. Crombie has suggested that religious language ought to be understood as parabolic.[14] The essence of a parable is to convey to us information about one reality by telling us about another reality. For instance, the real-

---

[14]I. M. Crombie in "Theology and Falsification," pp. 109–30.

ity that people respond variously to God's Word is illustrated by the parable which concerns itself with sowing seed. Crombie argues that we can never tell directly what God is like. If we begin with our conception of a human person and then strip away everything that does not apply to God, we are left with a mere "ghost of an image."[15] So, when we speak about divine realities, we need to talk in concrete terms which we know do not apply literally to God. These are parabolic. Parables provide concrete pictures, but we are aware that they are not to be taken as direct representations of God, for His essence is beyond our ken. To quote Crombie, "Statements about God, then, are in effect parables, which are referred, by means of the proper name, 'God,' out of our experience in a certain direction."[16]

Crombie attempts to combine the univocal and the equivocal. There is univocity in the known images of the parable. Equivocity arises out of the divine context; that is to say, the images do not literally apply. We cannot talk of the divine reality in itself. But then we are still in the realm of the equivocal, and have allowed no direct cognitive value for our parabolic discourse. Recognizing this fact, Crombie states that we accept the applicability of the parables on authority.[17] Still, an authorized or authoritative equivocity remains equivocity.

2. For Paul Tillich, religious language deals in symbols.[18] A symbol is like a sign in that it points away from itself to a further level of reality. But a symbol is also unlike a sign in that it participates in the reality toward which it points. Thus whereas a sign is part of one type of reality while it tells us about another, the symbol provides a bridge between the two levels. It picks us up on

[15]Ibid., p. 122.
[16]Ibid., p. 124.
[17]Ibid., p. 122.
[18]Paul Tillich, *Dynamics of Faith* (New York: Harper & Row, 1957), pp. 41–54.

one side and then propels us to the other side where a
different reality is disclosed to us. Religious language consists of various symbols which simultaneously speak to us
in mundane terms and disclose to us a spiritual reality of
which they are also part.[19] Thus the symbol is an analogical device. By bridging
two levels of reality it attempts to combine the univocal
and equivocal within itself. But again the specter of equivocity has not been purged. As Paul Edwards argued in
his scathing critique of Tillich,[20] unless one can reduce a
metaphor to some literal meaning, the metaphor is meaningless. And since Tillich's symbols disclose a spiritual
level which supposedly can never be spoken of directly,
we are faced with an irreducible metaphor which has no
meaning.

3. One of the most impressive attempts at explaining
religious language is that of Ian Ramsey.[21] Ramsey begins
with a concept of cosmic disclosure which is provided by
religious language. This disclosure is a sudden intuitive
awareness of reality seen in a brand new way. In order to
elicit this awareness, religious language uses models,
common everyday concepts, in talking of God. For instance, a personal model, such as "father," or an imper-
sonal one, such as "cause," can be applied to God. But
these models must be qualified. The qualifiers do not express a reality in themselves, but push onto the plane of
spiritual awareness. Thus we speak of "our father *in
heaven*" and the "*first* cause." Suddenly an infinite dimension has been introduced.[22]

Again we see the univocal (the models) combined with
the equivocal (the qualifiers). And once again we must

[19]Ibid., p. 46.
[20]Paul Edwards, "Professor Tillich's Confusions," *Mind* 74 (April, 1965):
197–206.
[21]Ian T. Ramsey, *Religious Language* (New York: Macmillan, 1957), and
*Christian Discourse* (New York: Oxford, 1965).
[22]Ramsey, *Christian Discourse*, pp. 66–90.

note that the result is ultimately still equivocity. Although Ramsey argues for the objectivity of religious language in providing a cosmic disclosure, it is clear that the cognitive value has been removed. Such a disclosure, regardless of its reality as a psychological experience, cannot give us genuine information about God and His will. Thus it would appear that theories of religious language which come under the heading of analogy are failures. Religious language remains equivocal. But this basic flaw is remedied by the concept of analogy which has come down to us by way of Aristotle and the Thomistic tradition.

*Thomistic Analogy*

What is missing in all of the above concepts of analogy is any notion of a positive correlation between the two levels of reality, the mundane and the divine.[23] If we begin with an unbridgeable gulf and the assumption that what is on the other side of the gulf is inherently unknowable, of course equivocity is the only possible result. But that assumption must be challenged.

Let us recall the whole context out of which this discussion arose, namely, the fact of revelation. We began to be puzzled about verbal revelation, but only after we had already established that God has revealed Himself concretely in history, beginning with creation. So we must learn this lesson from the advocates of catalogy, that ontologically God's creative and revelatory acts precede the linguistic order. Thus there is already a positive relationship between the mundane and divine based on God's initiative towards the world.

As a result, we can approach the topic of religious language with a metaphysical underpinning that eliminates the immediate slide back into equivocity which we witnessed above. God is not totally unknown to us. He is

[23]The following discussion relies heavily on E. L. Mascall, *Existence and Analogy* (London: Longmans, Green & Co., 1949), pp. 97–121.

known insofar as He has shown Himself. Then our language about God does not refer to something utterly alien, but to an object only partially known. It is perfectly plausible to say that one does know something partially without having to concede not knowing it at all.

So there is a partial knowledge of God available to us around which God-language is centered. This knowledge of God comes from His self-disclosure in creation and history. The facts of creation and history are this-worldly and, thus, conveyed to us by univocal language.

Consequently, we can construct a new type of analogy, one based on a positive creature-Creator relationship. We assume that any quality possessed by a creature is given to it by the Creator who possesses that quality (if it is a positive perfection) preeminently. Then we can take our human concepts of love, fatherhood, strength, and the like, and apply them to divine love, fatherhood, or strength, knowing that these concepts which apply to creatures apply to God with infinite perfection since He is their source. This is different from catalogy because we begin with the human term and extrapolate to the divine application. This type of analogy is referred to as analogy of attribution.

Let us see how this form of analogy compares to the other types previously mentioned. Once again we have a univocal element, bounded by the creaturely concept. Further, again there is equivocity since the concept is not of the same order when it applies to God. However, this time, because of our underlying metaphysical assumption, we know the univocal concept as a whole does apply to God, only to an infinite degree. There is no danger that the concept as a whole will not apply. In this form of analogy the equivocal element is not caused by God's sheer unknowability, but merely by man's incomplete knowledge of Him. Thus the analogy of attribution makes positive talk about God possible—but only on a proper metaphysical foundation.

The same reasoning applies to the second type of Thomistic analogy, analogy of proportionality. Here also the analogy is predicated on a positive correlation between creature and Creator. A typical example of analogy of proportionality is: "The love of the creature is to the nature of the creature as the love of God is to the nature of God." We know what human love is like from our human experience; we see its relationship to human nature. Then we infer that there must be an equal relationship between divine love and the divine nature.

Here again univocity is found in the linguistic expression of the creaturely experience. Equivocity comes into play when we realize that God's nature is infinitely greater than ours and only very imperfectly knowable. But recognizing that we are not left without clues about God, since He is Creator and Revealer, we can have confidence that our analogy of proportionality holds. Hence, even though we do not have univocal access to God, this analogy does supply a positive route to knowledge about Him via religious language.

But now we have come to a point where our metaphysical assumption must be further refined and explored. Specifically, we have shown that the possibility of religious language is dependent on the existential reality of a Creator-God. In the next chapter we will start to lay down the philosophical conditions for this conception of God.

# 7

# God

## *His Existence and Preeminence*

In our transcendental quest after the philosophical underpinnings of systematic theology, we have come to the point where it is necessary to discuss God and His nature. Here it becomes very difficult to select the proper issues to treat in a prolegomena. After all, so many books have been written about God, many of them philosophical, that it would be absurd to think that we can come close to doing justice to all of the issues involved. Nevertheless, some important points need to be made.

Our question, as usual, is transcendental: What are the philosophical concepts underlying the notion of God in orthodox theology? Our discussion will fall into two parts. In this chapter, we will discuss God's essential nature. In the next chapter, we will turn to God's relationship to the world in history.

### God as Necessary Existence

It is a well-known fact that the Bible presupposes the existence of God. Consequently, systematic theology should also presuppose His existence, for theology needs to remain as closely aligned to revelation as possible. But prolegomena is different. Unlike theology, which begins with God, prolegomena begins with man and studies the human categories which make theology possible. Here the philosophical question of whether there is a God cannot be avoided. So our first question in dealing with God has to be about His existence.

But even before we can properly ask this first question, another matter has to be settled. We need to decide who or what it is whose existence we are determining. This is certainly no trivial matter. Occasionally one hears it said of a certain argument for God's existence that it may be successful as an argument, but does not prove the existence of the biblical God.[1] From the theological point of view, it is the God of the Bible whose existence we are discussing. But philosophically, more needs to be said. On that level the questions of whether God exists and how to understand Him are inseparable, as we shall discuss presently.

Let us return for a moment to our prolegomena's starting point: man. We have described man in terms of his dual nature combining form and matter. Inherent in this understanding of man are certain limitations. His very historicity implies space and time limitations. The body, in addition, is subject to disease and decay. The mind cannot accomplish all it wants to. These are accidental limitations, that is, they come along with the nature of man as side effects.

But there is also an essential limitation to man, one which is inherent in his composite nature. Man is man only insofar as his form (spirit, soul, mind) is brought into conjunction with matter (body). A body by itself is only a dead mass of flesh, and the form considered alone indicates merely the potentiality to actualize a human being, should the form be filled out with matter. But it is not at all necessary that this combination be carried out. We can conceive of many a form which has never been conjoined

---

[1]Cf. Gordon H. Clark, "Revealed Religion," in *Fundamentals of the Faith*, ed. Carl F. H. Henry (Grand Rapids: Baker, 1969), p. 13.

with a material body, and which therefore does not exist: a unicorn, phoenix, or the pot of gold at the end of a rainbow, for example. For all of these entities, we know what they are like, but we also know that they do not have being. To put it into formal philosophical terms, their essence does not imply their existence.[2] Man is like those beings. Of course a major, nontrivial difference is that man does exist. But this difference is not inherent in man's essence. There could very well be an essence of man without a single man existing. The fact of man's existence is not necessary; his existence is contingent, that is, man could just as well not-be. Man, on his spiritual side, has an awareness of this fact; he refers to the dissolution of the unity between his form and matter as death. Still, the potential of death does not afford an adequate understanding of man's contingency. It is not just in the future, but at every moment of his existence, that it is true of man that he could just as easily not-exist, that his essence does not necessitate his actual being.

From this vantage point we can contrast man's perception of God. God is the Being that exists without limitations, and this lack of limits begins with His existence itself. God is the one whose essence is to exist. To understand God's nature, to talk about His essence, is to say that, if He exists at all, He exists necessarily, that is, He cannot not-exist.

So man, with his ever-present potential to cease existing, is thus distinct from God, for whom there is no such potential. In fact, God's existence need never be actualized. There is no potential in Him since He cannot come into being or cease to exist. In other words, God is pure actuality.

However, even though, given a proper understanding of God's essence, man recognizes Him as self-existent, this

[2]Thomas Aquinas, *On Being and Essence*, trans. Armand Maurer (Toronto: Pontifical Institute of Medieval Studies, 1968), p. 55.

fact is not intuitive for man. We stated above that, if God exists at all, He exists necessarily, but this requires that we first of all show that He exists. Fortunately this can be done while we speak to the mystery of man's existence. If it is not of man's essence to exist, yet man exists anyway, there must be a cause for man's existence. Unless there is a cause of man's existence, he will vanish into nothingness or never exist to begin with. We must keep before us that we are not referring just to man's coming into existence, but that his being, at every moment of time, hinges on the persistent actualization of his potential to exist. Once that cause of existence ceases, man ceases. An analogy might be the continuing flame of a Bunsen burner which depends on a steady supply of gas from outside of itself; once the supply is cut off, the flame ceases.

Just as a Bunsen burner does not cause its own flame, man cannot cause his own existence. If he did, he would have to exist as cause before he exists as effect, a patent absurdity. Man stands here as one example of all beings that exist even though their essence does not imply existence; this description includes the entire world. The world, the totality of all there is, need not exist, but it does. Modern modal logic is premised on the idea that this actual world is only contingent; there could have been many other possible worlds, including one in which nothing exists. Thus our question of why man exists becomes a more general question: why is there something rather than nothing, or why is there any contingent being? And the answer has to be: Because it is caused.

There are two reasons why the ultimate cause of contingent being cannot itself be contingent: (1) If it were, it would be contingent upon itself and we would be stuck with the logical impossibility of self-caused being. (2) No individual contingent entity can cause its own existence. Its potentiality must be actualized by another entity. But if the other also exists contingently, we are still in need of a source for its actuality. This argument can be stretched out into a line of causes all of which are contingent and thus stand in need of actualization of their existence. But regardless of how long this chain is, eventually it has to stop at one cause which exists necessarily; that is, at a cause whch contains no potentiality for existence which must be actualized. If we find no such cause, there is no transcendental possibility for any actual existence. Note that the philosophical description of a cause which contains no potential for existence needing to be actualized is what we earlier applied to God.[3]

Stripped of metaphysical technical expressions, this is what the argument amounts to: Man does not need to exist, yet he does. The mystery of his existence can be accounted for only on the basis that there is a God who is the cause of his existence. Thus we have here another typical transcendental argument: The existence of man is grounded in the existence of God.

That man is conscious of his contingency makes this argument easier to relate to. We can cite here Friedrich Schleiermacher's feeling of absolute dependence, Martin Heidegger's being-unto-death, or Jean-Paul Sartre's vision of the limitations of *être-pour-soi*. But though these ideas may enhance the plausibility of the argument, it must be emphasized that it does not rest on a consciousness or feeling, but on an ontological reality, the contingency of human existence.

In light of our remarks on faith and reason in chapter 4, we need not deal here with the argument that it is impossible to rationally demonstrate God's existence. All of what we said there applies here as a special case. If our argument in this section has succeeded, then its conclusion (God's existence) is clearly possible. If the argument

---

[3]For the record, the obvious indebtedness of this entire range of argumentation to Aquinas, *Summa Theologica*, I, q. 2, art. 3, needs to be mentioned. Of course this argument has been reproduced, altered, and attacked innumerable times.

did not work, we have not therefore impeached the possibility of His existence. Everything depends on the efficacy of the evidence, in this case the interpretation we give to the contingent existence of man. If that evidence does not suffice, our proof of God's existence is unconvincing, and the issue is not probable, but in doubt, insofar as it hinges on rational proof (of course, it need not). But if the evidence is sufficient, *ex post facto* haggling over theoretical possibilities is fatuous.

Now we need to return to the issue we touched on at the outset of this chapter, which represents a far more important question for our purposes. There is widespread controversy over the value of theistic arguments in relation to the God of the Bible. It is pointed out that the cosmological argument, for example, leaves us with an abstract entity, a First Cause, perhaps a god of the philosopher; but this deity is a long way from the personal Creator-God of the Scriptures. Our analysis of God's nature in the rest of this chapter, specifically His perfections and uniqueness, is intended to demonstrate that the philosopher and theologian do talk about the same God.

### God as Preeminent

We must here explore the philosophical basis for God's nature as the theologian conceives of it. It is one thing to assert God's existence; it is yet another to see Him as the Supreme Being. It is our contention that philosophy can here also provide an underpinning. This is done most handily by bringing up arguments first for God's supremacy, and then for His uniqueness.

It might appear at first that this will be either an extremely difficult task or an attempt to arbitrarily justify revelatory data. However, it is a fact that philosophy is on surprisingly self-sufficient grounds here. Once we have shown philosophically that God is an uncaused being, we can analyze that particular notion and then proceed to look at His nature and attributes.

*A Negative Approach to Knowledge of God's Attributes*

Let us again look at man and the dimensions of his existence. We have shown that man is essentially limited in that his very existence is contingent. And we also alluded to the fact that there are accidental limitations involved in his nature; that is, curtailments of his existence resulting from his being a creature restricted by space and time. These two types of limitation are correlated; both of them derive from the fact that man is a contingent unity of form and matter. Whatever existence and faculties man has, are brought about by his existential cause; they are not inherent. But this very causedness limits man at the same time as it endows him with his characteristics. Man can be only what his causes permit him to be.

Now contrast man with an uncaused, self-existent being. Such an entity is completely independent of any external causes. In the absence of any causation impinging on this being, it is free from the limitations concomitant with causedness. All causes limit in some way, and all limits can be understood as related to causes of some sort. Where there are no causes, there are no limits. Thus, when we think of God as uncaused and self-existent, we can also conceive of Him as completely unlimited.

Therefore, we can draw proper conclusions about God's nature by simply stating that He is free from those limitations which are placed on man. For instance, man is limited by space and time; God is free of those barriers, and we think of Him as ubiquitous and eternal. Man is stymied by his body; God is incorporeal. Man always has to cope with changes; God is immutable. There is no need to expand this list. The principle is clear: Whereas man is finite, God is infinite.

When we say that God is unlimited, we must be careful to remind ourselves that what we mean is that He is not limited by finite existence. There is no room here for the absurdity of God's somehow being free to contradict His own nature. He cannot cease to be God, cause His own existence, stop being loving, or make a stone so big that He cannot lift it. It is not that God is subject to the laws of logic (if He were, logic would be considered a God-behind-God); rather the laws of logic are part of His self-disclosure in creation. He cannot go against His own nature.

There is an immediate problem connected with this negative way of conceiving of God's attributes: Are we then saying anything about God at all? It could be argued that when one says what something is not, one has not said anything. For example, the statement, "My curtains are not green," seems to be vacuous since it does not tell us what color the curtains are. But the situation changes if we add that all other curtains are green. We still may not know what color the curtains are (and perhaps never will), but suddenly we have said something extremely significant: Here is one exception to the universal pattern in the color of curtains. These are the only curtains which are not green. Such a disclosure is in itself remarkable.

This is also the case for our negative approach to knowledge of God. Here we have one being that is totally immune from the limits of existence to which all other beings are subject. This is an extremely significant statement about this self-existent being.

It must be emphasized that we are not denying to God the very category of existence. There is a rather strong tradition, beginning in the neo-Platonism of Plotinus, which would say that God does not exist.[4] Plotinus, of course, was not a Christian; but his conception of the One was applied by Christian theologians in their view of God. Plotinus arranged Plato's Forms into a hierarchy. The cul-

[4]Plotinus, *Enneads* in *The Essential Plotinus*, trans. and ed. Elmer O'Brien (New York: Mentor, 1964), pp. 73–88.

mination of the hierarchy is the absolute unity of everything expressed in all the Forms, but this unity is not just
another Form. This Absolute, which Plotinus calls the One,
is beyond all the qualities which the Forms impart, including the category of existence as well. It is not possible
to say that the One exists, but neither is it permissible to
say that it does not exist. The One is simply beyond the
concept of existence.[5]

This neo-Platonic notion from Plotinus was frequently
accepted by Christian theologians and has persisted to
this day. A contemporary exponent of this view is Paul
Tillich, who argues that God is beyond the category of
existence.[6] To say that God exists is to place God among
all the creaturely entities with their limitations. Yet the
expression, "God exists," is not false; rather it is a symbol
which transcends the direct literal meaning it appears to
convey. The same principle applies to the expression, "God
does not exist." It is true insofar as it states that the category of existence does not apply to God, but it is false
insofar as it tries to conceive of Him in existential terms.
God is beyond existence and nonexistence.[7]

This approach has a certain appeal to it. It seems to be
one further step in the direction of severing God from all
connections with the limitations of finite existence. However, there are two basic problems:

1. We have to recognize a fundamental distinction between the notion of existence and the properties of an
existent being. This is the difference between essence and
existence we discussed earlier. We can know all the characteristics of an entity (e.g., of a unicorn or a man) without

[5]A quick glance at the writings of Plotinus in translation will certainly
reveal the fact that Plotinus did use the word *exists* of the One. But it should
also be clear that this is merely a convenient use of the term in passages
where some such term has to be used. The One is repeatedly stated to be
beyond all categories of being (Ibid., p. 80).

[6]Paul Tillich, *Systematic Theology* (Chicago: University of Chicago, 1951),
vol. 1, pp. 204–05.

[7]Paul Tillich, *Dynamics of Faith* (New York: Harper & Row, 1957), p. 48.

knowing whether it really exists or not. In the words of Immanuel Kant, "Existence is not a predicate."[8] When we say that something exists, Kant argues, we are not adding some property to a concept; we are indicating that there is an object corresponding to the concept. Thus existence is not one of the many properties which an object might possess.

Hence, when we define the attributes of God by stating that He is free from the limitations of man, there is no warrant for including the very notion of existence in the process. When we make an existential judgment, we are not defining nor adding properties or modes of existence; all we are doing is judging that these properties are instantiated in a being. Seen from this perspective, anything short of the affirmation of God's existence is inadequate for theology, which has, after all, God as its subject. To deny existence to God is not to exalt Him, but to deny Him altogether.

2. When we discuss different modes of existence (i.e., different essences), it is clear that God's existence is radically different from other existences. He exists without limit, whereas everything else exists with limits. It is here that we have to draw the line of distinction. But there is no warrant for construing unlimited existence as beyond existence.

*Positive Attributes*

Having taken this negative approach to describing the attributes of God, we are still left with a feeling that there is a lot more to be said about God. For one thing, Scripture gives a great amount of information about God which cannot be explained by simply stating that He is free of the limitations to which man is subject. We turn now to the question of whether these additional attributes can be derived philosophically.

[8]Immanuel Kant, *Critique of Pure Reason*, trans. Norman Kemp Smith (New York: St. Martin's, 1929), pp. 504–05.

Again we can start by focusing on the nature of man. We recognize in man many properties which we consider to be positive assets. For instance, human beings exemplify love, beauty, wisdom, and justice. It is true that no person possesses all of them perfectly, but they are there nonetheless.

We have already shown that God is the cause of man's existence. Now a cause cannot convey a property it does not possess; for example, an ice cube cannot start a forest fire. Hence, whatever properties God conveys to man's existence, He must possess Himself. Therefore, we can ascribe love, beauty, wisdom, and justice to God.

Incorporated in this argument is a concept of causality which may appear somewhat peculiar. Counterexamples quickly come to mind. You push a button; electricity flows from it to a bell; the bell rings; a loud sound is heard. The pushing of the button is the cause of the bell's ringing. But there is no sound in the pushing of the button or the electrical connection. Thus we have here a case where a cause does not possess the property it induces.

Now there is no point in attempting to reinterpret this counterexample. There is no ringing sound in the button, not even potentially. What we need to do in order to let our original argument stand is to distinguish between different types of causes and causal situations. Many causes do not convey any properties at all. They may be events which bring about further events, or they may be events or entities which actualize a property previously contained, not in themselves, but in the entities which they affect. The bell-ringing example falls into the latter category. But these descriptions do not exhaust all of the types of causes with which we are familiar. There are cases where causes do convey a property; for instance, in our original example, a forest fire must be actualized by some entity possessing the property of burning, such as a match or a spark.

Thus we are entitled to say that at least sometimes an

effect has a property which must also be part of the cause; else there is no effect. This is particularly true where a cause brings about the very existence of its effect. In such cases there is a convertible relationship between the properties of the cause and its effect. For example, a cat can progenerate only kittens, and a kitten must have a cat for its parent. The epitome of this kind of causality occurs when there is no set of antecedent conditions in which the cause operates; the cause by itself is the sum total of all necessary and sufficient conditions for the existence of the effect. Then the effect cannot contain any positive properties which are not directly traceable back to the cause. This is exactly the relationship between God, the cause, and man, the effect.

Of course God possesses these characteristics perfectly, whereas man has them in only a limited way. As the first, unlimited cause, God is not subject to the conditions which cause man to fall short of perfection in all these qualities. It is only analogically that we can predicate these positive qualities of God (cf. the discussion in chapter 6), but this is not to say that they are not legitimate predicates.

A natural objection against this view centers around the fact that in man we also recognize negative qualities: hate, ugliness, stupidity, injustice. Must we therefore also predicate these qualities of God? If so, our philosophical underpinning of Christian theology is certainly in trouble. But a quick analysis of these qualities shows that we are safe. What these, and other similar negative characteristics, amount to is a lack of positive qualities. Hate is the absence of love; ugliness is the absence of beauty; and so forth. The negation of an effect is not a property we need to trace back to the cause. Thus, metaphysically speaking, God need not be seen as causally conveying these qualities to man. On the contrary, since His existence is not limited, we know that He cannot be limited in His possession of the positive properties, limitation in which amounts to the negative properties in man.

But what about the many other human attributes which, though not negative, would be frivolous if applied to God? We may say of a human being that he or she is blond, a vegetarian, and athletically inclined. To say these things of God would be theologically inappropriate. In dealing with this issue, note, first of all, that insofar as these properties presume a physical body, they are ruled out, as we decided already that God is incorporeal. Second, we need to emphasize that the properties which can be traced back to God are *positive* in character. Accidental qualities, the possession of which is indifferent to an entity, need not be located in God as their direct source. This line of reasoning very obviously involves a somewhat arbitrary judgment as to what are positive properties as opposed to accidental ones. But this can be admitted freely, for ability to draw up a tight list of which qualities can be attributed to God, and which cannot, is not a requisite for our argument to hold for at least the theologically conventional properties.

A word needs to be said to distinguish this form of argumentation from the thought of Ludwig Feuerbach.[9] Feuerbach argued in a similar vein that the attributes man assigns to God are perfect representations of the positive qualities of man. But for Feuerbach, God is merely the psychological projection of an idealization of man. God, for him, actually does not exist. He is a fiction created by man as a repository for everything that is good about man. Our approach is diametrically opposed to that way of thinking. We are basing our analysis on the fact that God really exists and that as Creator He has endowed man with His positive qualities. Thus there is no similarity between our metaphysical view of God as First Cause and Feuerbach's view of God as projection.

[9]Ludwig Feuerbach, *The Essence of Christianity*, trans. George Eliot (New York: Harper & Row, 1957).

## God as Unique

Finally, we must show that there is only one God to whom we ascribe this nature. Once again the starting point of our argument is man. Why is there more than one person? Because there is more than one unity of body and spirit in existence, each one possessing particular characteristics. If two persons had the same body and spirit and all the same properties, we would actually have only one person. On a similar basis, let us see if it is possible to have two Gods. Of course what applies to two applies to more than two *a fortiori*.

Since, as we have said, God does not have a body, bodies cannot serve as individuating criteria. All that is left is spirit along with certain properties. Can these properties be used to distinguish between Gods?

At first glance, it seems quite plausible to conceive of a God who has certain properties and of a second God who may have certain other properties which serve to set Him apart. However, the question must be raised as to whether a God who lacks a certain quality which He might have had as God, is God at all. The answer is clearly no; for the absence of such a property would imply a limitation which cannot apply to God as First Cause. Only a God who has all of the properties which He might conceivably possess is God. Hence there cannot be two Gods; since, if God possesses all the qualities He might possess, there is no criterion for individuation. Two Gods with all the same qualities are the same God.[10]

The same point can be made along a slightly different line, utilizing a principle derived from Gottfried Leibniz's doctrine of the identity of indiscernibles. We begin with

[10]This argument has been around the philosophical world in various guises at least since the time of Parmenides. It has most recently been revived by Norman Geisler, *Philosophy of Religion* (Grand Rapids: Zondervan, 1974), pp. 205–07.

the premises that two individuals are identical if they share the same set of properties and that there are certain properties a being must possess in order to be God. Now suppose there are two beings each claiming to be God. Either they do not share the same properties (i.e., they are discernible), in which case one must be deficient in divine properties; or they share all the same properties, in which case they are indiscernible and, hence, identical.

This last argument ought to be sufficient to finally lay to rest the problem which has been looking over our shoulder all along: the alleged difference between the god of philosophy and the God of the Bible. Not only have we shown that God is supreme, but in this last section we have also argued that conceptually there can be only one supreme being. This argument must apply to the God of the Bible. If He is supreme, then conceptually He cannot be a different supreme being from the one that philosophy shows to exist. Certainly philosophy and Scripture have different interests and emphases, but this gives us no right to therefore stipulate two different supreme beings.

Thus far our analysis has provided only one very abstract way of understanding God. Theology posits that this God not only created the world, but is active in it. The next chapter will explore in more detail the relationship of God to the world.

# 8

# God and History

The last chapter was occupied with a contrast between God and man, showing the exaltedness of God—God as self-existent, preeminent, and unique. Such a description of God may lead to the position that God is so remote that He has no tangible relations with the world. But the view that God is isolated from the world is extremely problematic.

Christian theology has traditionally held that there are two elements to God's relationship to the world: His transcendence and His immanence. His transcendence refers to His separation from the world, His otherness. But His immanence must not be ignored; God is revealed to be present and acting in the world. This second element introduces a polarity that has become one of the most ticklish problems in theology: how to reconcile God's transcendence and immanence.

Much of the preceding discussion has been predicated on the self-disclosure of God in history, the revelational datum for which we now need to provide some philosophical categories. There are two particular problems which arise out of this issue. We need to come to terms with, first, the question of God's relationship to time, and, second, the question whether He changes with the flow of time. Unless we can provide some clear answers to these two questions, we cannot conceptualize God's relationship to our history and, consequently, to the world. In practice, these issues are rather intertwined and are usually treated together. We shall follow suit.

A pacesetting contribution in this area was made by Oscar Cullmann in *Christ and Time*. From an analysis of the concepts of time in the New Testament, Cullmann came to the following conclusions:

1. Biblical revelation is inherently historical. Cullmann states that "all Christian theology in its innermost essence is Biblical history."[1] This history is linear, in contrast to the Greek circular conception. At the midpoint of history stands Jesus Christ in whom we see the "already and not yet," that is, both the accomplished and anticipated elements of redemption history.

2. The Bible does not recognize an eternity of timelessness. That notion is a later philosophical one. "Thus in the New Testament field it is not time and eternity that stand opposed, but limited time and unlimited, endless time. . . . Eternity is the endless succession of the ages."[2]

3. God is Lord over time. This does not imply that God is independent of time, but rather that He is in control of it. We see that "God alone rules over time, for he alone can survey it in its entire extension."[3]

Cullmann's analysis of salvation history and God's place therein, though not beyond criticism,[4] provides a good description of the New Testament understanding of time. But we must realize that Cullmann is not speaking directly to the problem we have posed in this chapter. He is working on the level of biblical, rather than systematic, theology. Cullmann has provided us with a very clear pic-

---

[1]Oscar Cullmann, *Christ and Time*, rev. ed., trans. Floyd V. Filson (Philadelphia: Westminster, 1964), p. 23.

[2]Ibid., pp. 46, 62.

[3]Ibid., p. 79.

[4]See James Barr, *Biblical Words for Time* (Naperville, IL: Alec R. Allenson, 1962).

ture of the historical involvement of God in the history of revelation. But he has not shown us how the philosophical concept of an eternal God can be made to fit into that biblical framework. Cullmann does not consider this question improper; rather he sees it as beyond his concern in understanding the New Testament.[5] We, however, must pursue it.

At the time of this writing, this issue is one of the most volatile ones in theology. Much debate is carried on about it. The fact that philosophical presuppositions are of tantamount importance is increasingly obvious. Thus this is fertile ground for a study in prolegomena. Our approach in this chapter will be to present several contrasting views on the subject, attempt respective critiques, and take some steps in the direction of a synthesis.

## Alternative Views of God and Time

*Augustine: God as the Eternal Now*

Augustine of Hippo will be our first representative thinker. He is an advocate for the tradition which sees God far removed from the world and its temporality. God, for Augustine, is totally above the flux of time and change.[6]

Time, says Augustine, is a by-product of creation. Only the creature experiences the succession of changes which are measured by time. And only the present moment is real. What we call past and future are essentially products of the mind as it remembers and projects. But actual experience can be only of present moments. One cannot experience something that is no longer here or that is not yet real.[7]

Whereas man can know only a succession of moments

---

[5]Cullmann, *Christ and Time*, p. 11.

[6]Augustine, *Confessions*, trans. John K. Ryan (Garden City, NY: Doubleday, 1960), pp. 277–304.

[7]Ibid., p. 301.

which appear as novelties and vanish never to be realized again, God is not subject to this flux. God is free of the barriers which impose their limitations on us. God knows the future as well as the past exhaustively. Consequently, there is no future or past for Him. He exists in a state in which what we call past and future are just as present to Him as our present moments. All three divisions of time are experienced by Him simultaneously. Thus for God all of time is the one present moment, the eternal now. We see here then the traditional distinction between time and eternity, where God, immune from all temporality, is a truly eternal being. Eternity implies complete timelessness, not merely existing everlastingly in time.[8]

Thus God is in no way subject to time or changes. The time sequence of God's acts in history is merely an accommodation to our perspectives. We can see things only in a temporal framework which does not exist from God's bird's-eye view.

We see here in Augustine a typically neo-Platonic perception of God. Now Augustine himself was too level-headed a theologian to let this understanding impair his conception of God's acts in history. But the seeds of a theological problem are here, and can lead to a misunderstanding which isolates God in a temporal antisepsis. God has, as it were, taken the place of Plotinus's One. He is totally removed from the categories within which the world exists. Consequently, the world takes on a quality of unreality; man's perception of the world is based on the illusion of temporality. This is normal for a Platonic metaphysics, where the existent world gives way to the higher reality of the Forms. For Augustine, the Forms are the Eternal Ideas in the mind of God.

This misunderstanding of God and time (it is also a misrepresentation of Augustine inasmuch as it focuses only on his Plotinian roots) is detrimental to the conception of

---

[8]Ibid., pp. 303-04.

man and revelation which has arisen out of our previous discussions. It gives the historical events of God's self-revelation second-rate status in contrast to the higher eternal realities. This view speaks to the Platonic conception of man as primarily spiritual. But as soon as we take the materiality and historicity of man into consideration, it becomes inadequate. A conception of revelation grounded in history must see the historical events as more than accommodations bordering on illusion.

### Barth and Bultmann: God in His Own Time

Despite their many profound differences, Karl Barth and Rudolf Bultmann share some very similar conceptions when it comes to understanding temporality and God. Their viewpoint is similar to, yet different from, Augustine's.[9] What Barth and Bultmann take over from Augustine's Platonic notions, and in fact amplify, is the idea that common history is not revelatory of God. History (Bultmann's *Historie*)[10] is a succession of temporal events which can serve to convey eternal truths only indirectly.

Bultmann takes steps that Augustine would never have permitted, such as denying any particular significance to the historical event of the resurrection.[11] Its real significance lies in the faith-event.

The basic difference from Augustine lies in the fact that

[9]Rudolf Bultmann, *Kerygma and Myth*, ed. Hans Werner Bartsch (New York: Harper & Row, 1953), pp. 34–43; Karl Barth, *Church Dogmatics*, III. 2, trans. Harold Knight, G. W. Bromiley, J. K. S. Reid, and R. H. Fuller (Edinburgh: T. & T. Clark, 1960), pp. 437–640.

[10]Bultmann, *Kerygma*, p. 37.

[11]Ibid., pp. 38–43. Barth would never say such a thing, of course. He insists that the Christian message is grounded in history and that the resurrection is the epitome of this revelation. However, it would be misleading on this basis to interpret Barth as not making a distinction between our time and God's time. God's own time, the time of Jesus Christ, takes precedence over human and mundane time. And salvation history is ultimately based on God's time. Thus, even though Barth insists on the reality and historicity of the resurrection, it is in the last analysis not on a par with other historical occurrences. See *Church Dogmatics*, III. 2, pp. 455–56, and also 473–74.

Barth and Bultmann do not confine God to the state of the eternal now (in contrast to creaturely time). Instead they insist that God has His own time, which is different from ours. This time is expressed in *Geschichte*, the history of salvation as it unfolds for our redemption. *Geschichte* is not dependent on *Historie* with its contingent facts. This is the sphere in which God has passed His decrees and enacted salvation for us.[12]

This approach only aggravates the problem. It affirms the Platonic gulf between God and man. In attempting to explain how the eternal God can be involved with a temporal revelation, providing God with His own temporality is of no help, since, under that hypothesis, God's history has no relation to man's history. Like two parallel lines which never meet, the two histories may run on and on without ever intersecting. It should be mentioned that Barth's (and to some extent, Bultmann's) christological solution is of no help here, since his Christology and soteriology are part of God's time, and not of our history.[13]

*Jürgen Moltmann: God of the Future*

The answer to the foregoing difficulties might lie in a reversal of hermeneutical procedure. Perhaps the best approach is to begin with the fact of historicity, apply it to God, and let traditional conceptions of God be altered to allow for temporality if need be. Such is the approach taken by our next two representatives.

In the 1960s the theology of Jürgen Moltmann was one

---

[12]Bultmann, *Kerygma*, p. 37; Barth, *Church Dogmatics*, III. 2, pp. 558–59.

[13]One must be careful not to regard some of Barth's statements as more helpful than they really are. For one thing, Barth's conception of the "eternity" of God is not the same as Augustine's, for in Barth God does experience the succession of events in His time (though certainly without beginning or end and in a way different from the way we experience time). Redemption history for Barth is ultimately not a confrontation between God and man (pace the dialectic of the *Epistle to the Romans*), but an event involving God the Father and the Son, Jesus Christ, the God-man.

of several reactions against Barth and Bultmann.[14] Moltmann came under the spell of the Marxist philosopher, Ernst Bloch, who gave him a new understanding of the future and Christian theology. Ernst Bloch is a Marxist, but not a dialectical materialist.[15] His thought is based on the Marxist notion of a future utopia, the classless society; but it is animated by a spiritual framework. Man, to Bloch, is more than an economic, material being. He is spiritual as well, with a soul and even the capability of becoming divine. The watchword of Bloch's philosophy is, "Erit sicut Deus—you shall become like God."[16]

The future tense of this slogan must be noted. Man has not attained divinity yet. The utopia has not yet arrived. For the moment, man is in a state of expectation; he is looking for something new and different to happen. Bloch has described the logic of his philosophy as "S is not yet P." This is intended to convey the thought that nothing is rigid; there is always the hope of a *novum* in the future.[17]

Moltmann finds this philosophy singularly suitable to express the truths of Christian eschatology. The Christian always lives within the framework of God's promise which will be fulfilled in the future parousia of Jesus Christ. Thus the Christian lives with exactly that kind of attitude of hope in the future that Bloch talks about. We must always be ready for the future and the novelties it will bring as we proceed towards the fulfilment of God's promises.[18]

[14]Jürgen Moltmann, *Theology of Hope*, trans. James W. Leitsch (New York: Harper & Row, 1967).

[15]Ernst Bloch, "Geist der Utopie," trans. John Cummings as "Karl Marx, Death and the Apocalypse" in *Man on His Own*, ed. J. Moltmann and R. Strunk (New York: Herder & Herder, 1970), p. 37.

[16]Ernst Bloch, *Tübinger Einleitung in die Philosophie*, vol. 2, reprinted in *Man on His Own*, p. 114.

[17]See Harvey Cox, "Ernst Bloch and the Pull of the Future," in *New Theology*, ed. Martin E. Marty and Dean G. Peerman (New York: Macmillan, 1968), vol. 5, pp. 191–203.

[18]"Within the historical *novum*, there lives the *Novum Ultimum*" (Ernst Bloch, quoted in Jürgen Moltmann, *Perspektiven der Theologie* [Munich: Kaiser, 1968], p. 196).

Of course, the distinction from Bloch, and not a minor one, is that Moltmann is not an atheist, but a Christian who believes in God and Jesus Christ. Being tied to the parousia of Jesus Christ, the future hope of the Christian is the future of Christ Himself. And further, as it is in this process that God fulfils His promise, it is also the future of God Himself. Thus God is linked to man's history through the category of the future. He works along with us in our temporal condition.[19]

In this way of looking at God temporality is the starting point. We begin by positing history, a new future, and a God who is part of that future. At the same time, Moltmann is not throwing out traditional theology; he does see the element of constancy in God. But it is a constancy expressed in His dealing with man through the pattern of promise and fulfilment.[20]

The main problem with Moltmann's view of God and history is its ontological vagueness. The always ongoing flux of his history with the constant potential for something new and different leaves us breathless looking for patterns that provide perspective on the scope of history. Moltmann does not allow for an underlying core or similarity in history. Consequently we cannot know what the parousia will be like. And for this reason we do not know God apart from the flow of history either. There is, then, no theology proper, only a theology of God-in-history.

But these conclusions are inadequate in the light of the ideas of the previous chapter. The contrast between God and creation must be maintained. One may not sacrifice the basic consideration of God's preeminence for the sake of preserving His historicity. For Moltmann there is no distinction between God in Himself and as He relates to the world. This appears to curtail God's unlimitedness.

[19]Moltmann, *Theology of Hope*, p. 16.
[20]Ibid., p. 104.

The greatest difficulty with Moltmann is that he leaves these issues too much in doubt.

### John Cobb: A Finite, Temporal God

John Cobb begins his theology with the assumption of modernity: Contemporary secular man has outgrown the principles of traditional theology.[21] Chief among these is the view of God as eternal Creator, Lawgiver, and Judge. Cobb finds such notions of God at best misleading, but more likely pernicious in their effect of turning modern man, who does not comprehend them, away from God. The old view of God has to be replaced by an approach suited to modern man, one in which God and man are seen as cooperating and suffering together.[22]

Cobb argues that the common experience of mankind provides such a concept of God. We experience a "call forward," a feeling that there is an ideal beyond us. This ideal must have objectivity; it is best understood along the lines of the philosophical model of God proposed by Alfred North Whitehead.[23]

Whitehead's metaphysics is based, not on static substances, but on the idea of events. Everything in the world is composed of occasions which combine both temporal and spatial aspects. Occasions can change from one moment to the next. The novelty in a new occasion must have been present potentially in the previous one. Therefore each event is bipolar, consisting of an actual pole and a potential pole. In each change, the potential pole is actualized.[24]

But such change is certainly not random. The world, which consists of occasions, represents a unified whole in which changes occur more or less according to well-es-

---

[21]John B. Cobb, Jr., *God and the World* (Philadelphia: Westminster, 1969).

[22]Ibid., pp. 19–41.

[23]Ibid., pp. 42–86.

[24]Alfred North Whitehead, *Process and Reality* (New York: Free Press, 1978), p. 45.

tablished patterns. For this reason, Whitehead posits a set of ideals (forms) that provide the necessary patterns. But these ideals do not exist in themselves; they exist in God.[25]

God, according to Whitehead, is no exception to the metaphysical rule of bipolarity. It is with His actual pole that God presents the ideals to the world. This pole is called God's consequent nature. But there is also a potential pole, His primordial nature. With His consequent nature God relates to the world; His primordial nature provides the ways in which God can potentially do this.[26]

Now this relationship between God and the world is not one of efficient cause and effect. God does not force the world to conform to the ideals. Rather, He presents the ideals as goals toward which the world should strive. God attempts to entice the world to follow His directions. In the last analysis, the world can always refuse to follow God's suggestions. Thus God is limited with regard to His influence on the world.[27]

A further limitation on God is that God cannot present the world with any patterns other than those which are permitted by the existent world configuration. Just as a chess player's strategy is determined by the set-up of the pieces on the board, so God cannot go beyond the way the world is at present. Hence God cannot predict the future; He has big plans for the future of the world (just as the chess player is working towards mating his opponent), but He can accomplish His plans only if the world cooperates.[28]

We can see now why Cobb insists that we can never talk about God by Himself. Though God is not identical with the world, He is not separate from it either. God and the world are always together in this process panenthe-

[25]Alfred North Whitehead, *Religion in the Making* (New York: World, 1926), p. 88.

[26]Whitehead, *Process*, pp. 31–34.

[27]Ibid., p. 32.

[28]Cobb, *God and the World*, pp. 87–102.

ism. Consequently all of the temporal limitations of the world apply to God as well. God is totally tied up with—yes, even dependent on—human history.[29]

There are numerous criticisms that can be leveled against process theology, beginning with questions of what constitutes revelation right on through many details in systematic theology. But we shall focus on a few points relevant to our present discussion.

1. The process view of God presents us with a novel conception. It certainly stands in contrast to all traditional theology with its emphasis on God's supremacy, omnipotence, and so on. To the extent that the process view is not the kind of theology for which we are writing this prolegomena, we are at liberty to ignore it.

But there are obviously issues here which come into the domain of our prolegomena. We must question the whole methodology on which process thought is based. It begins with an assumption about the pervasiveness of modern secularity. On the basis of that assumption it discards traditional theology. From there it turns to a philosophy which is more in keeping with the initial assumption and lets this philosophy determine theological content. Finally, to whatever extent Scripture is dealt with at all, it is accommodated to the philosophical theology.

This methodology and the role which philosophy plays here differ markedly from what we proposed in the first chapter. We argued that theology begins with an authoritative revelation from God, and that philosophy can be only a secondary means of expressing the content of revelation. Philosophy may never dictate theological content. Yet in process thought philosophy takes on this imperialistic role. Writers like John Cobb, Schubert Ogden,[30] and others begin with their arbitrary ratiocinations which may

---

[29]Ibid., pp. 80–84.
[30]Schubert Ogden, *The Reality of God* (New York: Harper & Row, 1977).

or may not be philosophically sound; the point is that theology apart from a revelational starting point can be only philosophy of religion or religious wisdom. The crucial foundation is missing.

2. Not much needs to be said about how this temporal view of God conflicts with the philosophical description of God in the previous chapter. The point is obvious. But it must be added that the process view is also philosophically impossible. We established in that chapter that finite being must be caused by something outside of itself, since a potential existence can never actualize itself. This impossibility is not logical, but metaphysical. The root of potentiality lies in dependence for existence on an outside cause. Such dependence is the very meaning of metaphysical potentiality. Yet in process theology we are presented with a God who has a potential pole which is supposed to actualize itself into the consequent nature. But without a cause this is impossible. Hence we are left with either a metaphysically absurd God, or we must posit a "God-behind-God," who actualizes God's potential. In either case we have a *reductio ad absurdum* refutation of process-theology proper.[31]

3. Our prolegomena shares a certain amount of philosophical ground with process theology in that it (though not the theology it is intended to support) also begins with man in his temporal experience. But whereas process thought goes on to define theology in those terms, we are using an anthropological starting point for a transcendental argument establishing the nature of divine revelation. This leads to the question of how we are to understand the relationship between an eternal God and a temporal world. Making God part of this temporality does not solve the problem; it merely explains away the problem and substitutes a very questionable metaphysics.

[31]Cf. Norman L. Geisler, *Christian Apologetics* (Grand Rapids: Baker, 1976), pp. 208–12.

It may help at this point to bring up a very important distinction between future-oriented theologies (e.g., Moltmann) and process thought (e.g., Cobb). Moltmann's God is temporal, but He is in charge of time and history. On the other hand, Cobb's God is temporal and at the mercy of history. Whereas in Moltmann we see God issue a promise which He personally will bring to fulfilment, Cobb can give no assurance as to the outcome of history. In fact, Cobb's history may have no outcome. Process theology presents us with a potentially never-ending temporal sequence which God can only endow with at best probable goals; He Himself has no assurance as to the realization of His plans. Moltmann, on the other hand, knows that the parousia is the certain end of history.

Now Cobb's understanding of history is hardly commensurate with the biblical view. This is not to make the issue revolve around to what extent he accepts as literal the biblical accounts. Rather the question is whether he even shares the basic biblical perspective that history has a beginning, middle, and end. Cobb, in keeping with his secularist assumptions, must bow to the secularist understanding of history as nothing more than an interminable progression of events. This is a possible understanding of history in keeping with a very rudimentary definition of historicity. Nonetheless, it is inferior in its theological potential as a vehicle for divine revelation. If we opt for a more stringent definition of "historical," perhaps a more conventional one under which history entails a meaningful plan of events, then Cobb's God may be temporal, but not historical. In short, a position like Cobb's is not at all helpful for understanding God's revelation to man in history. It fails in both its understanding of God and its concept of history.

## Synthesis: Eternity and History

We have looked at four alternatives for understanding God and history. The first two were inadequate because they isolated God too much from our time, the second pair because they made God part of time at the expense of His preeminence. We are clearly still in need of an adequate scheme.

At this point it may be tempting to take refuge in a concept of paradox, mystery, or the like. One could simply say that, since Scripture affirms both the eternity of God and His acts in history, all we need to do is affirm both as well without regard to whether the two can be philosophically reconciled. This approach is commendable for its recognition of scriptural revelation as primary authority, but from the standpoint of philosophical prolegomena it begs the question. If we are trying to supply a philosophical framework for systematics, we cannot abandon the project the first time we hit upon a serious problem. This is not to say that we need to have satisfactory explanations for every mystery in Christian theology. But we must remember that this very problem is of our own making, beginning with our philosophical description of God.

Let us see, then, if we can come up with a philosophical understanding of God and time, using, as always, a transcendental argument. The given for which we want to supply a philosophical account is twofold: God is unlimited (and therefore eternal), and He acts within time. Can we supply philosophical conditions which make this given conceptually possible?

Once again, let us return to our starting point, man. Our argument in the previous chapter ran like this: Man is a finite being whose contingent existence needs to be grounded in the necessary existence of God. The difference between these two modes of existence is that, whereas man is limited, God is not limited. One of the limitations on man to which God is not subject is time. To this extent it is quite correct to agree with Augustine that God is eternal, that is, completely timeless.

Now we need to remind ourselves that this entire metaphysical scheme is based on a positive relationship between God and man. They are not opposed to each other as polarities, but man stands open to God as creature to Creator, hearer to speaker, effect to cause. Thus we see that our very model already entails a causal relationship between God and the world. God is here seen as directing Himself outward to the world. But is this compatible with our exalted view of God?

We must realize that we came to God philosophically by way of the causal model, and that we cannot abscind the feature of causality from God. God, as we have come to know Him, is already in the act of causing the external existence of another. It is from this concept of His causality that we derived His attributes as unlimited. But then His attributes may not be seen as isolating God from the world in a sphere of remoteness. It is not necessary to identify God with the Plotinian One once we have established His necessary existence.

But even further, the very notion of necessary existence, if rightly understood, precludes an isolationist view of God. Necessary existence, we said, implies that there is in God no potentiality to exist, since He cannot not-be. Hence we must think of God as pure actuality of existence. Now this means that we cannot think of God as being subject to change, but it does not mean that pure actuality cannot be thought of as acting. In all finite beings, to act means to change, for in every case it implies the actualization of a certain potentiality. But infinite being is an exception here. When all actuality is already present, there is no need to actualize a potential. To the contrary, a purely actualized being can be understood as constantly acting.[32]

Still this neat metaphysical scheme seems to fall apart once we apply it to a particular example. Let us analyze, say, the idea of God speaking (ignoring whatever meaning one may want to read into that expression). It would ap-

---

[32]I have directed this line of argument against a hasty appropriation of Hegelian metaphysics in "Hegelian Themes in Contemporary Theology," *Journal of the Evangelical Theological Society* 22 (1979): 351–61.

pear that before God spoke, His speech was there potentially; then when He did speak, it became actual. Or, to
use an even more powerful example, before God caused
the world, He could potentially cause it, and by causing
it to exist, He actualized this potentiality in Himself. But
this objection has things backwards: it is not God who
exists first potentially and then actually, but His speech
and the world, both of which derive their existence from
Him.

Nonetheless, we seem to continue to be saddled with
the problem of God's performing an act after not having
performed it; therefore He must be a temporal God. In
order to solve the problem, we need to make it plausible
that an eternal God can act temporally, without either
the eternal or temporal element being somehow illusory.
In a Plotinian view (e.g., our misrepresentation of Augustine) God's eternality is genuine and His acts only appear
to be temporal. In Moltmann, God is not called eternal
apart from the connotations of His temporal acts. Can
this apparent dilemma be resolved?

To begin answering this question, it may be useful to
analyze the notion of temporality a little further. We have
been treating it as an attribute, a property of an entity.
But, strictly speaking, it is not so much a part of the entity
itself, but a condition under which an entity exists. It is
almost a category mistake to say that a being is round
and temporal. The roundness is part of the makeup of the
being, but the temporality is a condition, a limitation
which is imposed on it externally. If we see temporality
as a condition of existence rather than as a property, we
may begin to get a handle on our problem.

To illustrate this point, let us look at a nontheological
example. Imagine a man is watching a play on a television
set. He perceives the moving pictures and sounds that
represent the characters, scenery, and actions of the play.
These perceptions are, however, confined to the limits of
the television set. Yet in actuality the entire room is filled

with the electromagnetic waves which produce the play on the television. Thus the play is actually present in two modes, or under two different conditions. It is there on the television set under the conditions which have made it perceptible to the man. In this case it is visible and audible. But the play is also there in the form of the waves. And in this case there are no colors and no sound. The man cannot know it is there without a picture tube. But under these very different conditions, it is there nonetheless. This example could be expanded to include at least two other conditions under which this play exists—as the actors actually perform it on the sound stage, and as it is captured on the celluloid of the film which is later broadcast to the television set.

The point of analogy intended here is that something can occur under two very different conditions of existence without either form having to be considered illusory. Just as the play is real in two ways, as the electromagnetic waves and as the reproduction on television, so God's actions are real in two ways, in the temporal sequence as we perceive them in this world under creaturely conditions, and in their eternal reality in God Himself. It would be a big mistake for us to go beyond this statement, either somehow criticizing the notion of God's eternal actions or attempting to reduce it to more intelligible terms. From our point of view the idea of atemporal action is an absurdity, but we can affirm its truth without being able to conceive it, just as we can affirm all of God's lack of limitations without corresponding univocal concepts—by way of analogy.

Thus we can conclude by saying that God's temporal acts are real; God truly acts. Simultaneously it is true that the temporal sequence in which we see God's actions is not part of the conditions under which God Himself performs the actions. Both concepts—an eternal God and His temporal acts—are equally valid and real and are plausible without arbitrarily resorting to mystery or paradox.

The force of most of the preceding argumentation was directed against the view which isolates God in a remote eternity and lets His actions appear as illusory. But we must guard against the other extreme as well. We have made statements to the effect that it is part of God's very nature to act. God is pure act; philosophically we know Him only as the acting, causing One. But this description would seem to imply that God is constrained to act, or that He relates to the world from necessity.

The key here lies in the understanding of necessity. There is a certain kind of existential necessity which does not have the force of logical necessity. An example of this kind of necessity is found in my own existence, perhaps in an argument similar to Descartes's *cogito*. It would be absurd for me to deny my own existence, even though the sentence "I exist" is not true from logical necessity in the way that the sentence "I am I" is. We can understand God's relationship to the world as an existential necessity. Since this is the only way in which we can understand God and His actions in relation to the world, it cannot be denied. But we also understand from our earlier deliberations that God as God is free from all constraint and that, therefore, He acts freely. Consequently we do know that there is no logical necessity on God to act. God is free to act or not to act, and He is free to act in whatever mode He chooses. However, once He has acted, it is impossible to deny that He has acted, and that He has done so in a particular way. Once He established a relationship to the world which He created, He could not be thought of apart from the world. Nonetheless, we keep in mind that He freely established that relationship, not out of need or necessity, but out of His creative will.

We have investigated whether the idea of an eternal God revealing Himself in history does not involve an absurdity. We have tried to show that the notion of the timeless God freely acting within His temporal creation is philosophically sound. Now we need to become more specific. Christian theology maintains that God's revelation was epitomized in the fact that God Himself became man in history in Jesus Christ. The next chapter will explore several philosophical presuppositions of this assertion.

# 9

# God Revealed in Jesus Christ

"What philosophical concepts are necessary to allow us to understand the doctrines of Christology properly?" is the transcendental question of this chapter. Once again the theological data are decisive; the prolegomena attempts to facilitate their conceptualization. The sum of these data is that Jesus Christ has been revealed in history as both God and man. The theologian as exegete must support this claim; here we merely need to abet its intelligibility, not establish its facticity.

## Models of the Incarnation

Our first problem arises from the fact that in Jesus Christ we have one person who is both man and God. Such a statement seems at first to be self-contradictory. After all, we have gone to great lengths to emphasize the difference between God and man. God is a unique, self-existent, noncorporeal spirit; man is a limited, contingent, form-and-body unity. How can one person be both? Before presenting our solution, we will review several other models that have been proposed.

Let us return to our conceptualization of man as a unit of form (soul) and matter (body). Applying this concept to Christ, some of the earliest Christian thinkers substituted the Spirit or the *Logos* for the human soul. Whereas other men consist of a human soul indwelling a human body, Jesus is a divine "soul" indwelling a human body.[1] Thus both the divine and human aspects are taken care of, and a certain unity has been preserved.

But this model suffers in both its theology and its anthropology on Platonic and Aristotelian presuppositions alike. If we were to buy into the Platonic anthropology of an autonomous soul inhabiting a dispensable body, the only significant component in the christological model would be the divine soul. The body would not be important for by itself it cannot constitute humanity. Since under this scheme the human soul would be missing, Christ would not be truly human at all.

In an Aristotelian anthropology the form determines the body. Hence, if we substitute a divine form for the human one, we are left with one of three unacceptable options:

1. The body is truly human; the form truly divine. Then the body is somehow human without the form of humanity, a metaphysical impossibility.
2. The form is truly divine, determining the body. Then the body cannot be human. It must be a divine body (Apollinarianism). This is a lesser form of the heresy of Docetism—that Jesus was human in appearance only.
3. The body is truly human, determined by its form. Then the form cannot be divine, a notion contrary to our presupposition.

In short, any Christology which tries to substitute the divine spirit for the human soul is inadequate. In order to preserve both divinity and humanity, we must main-

[1]John N. D. Kelly, *Early Christian Doctrines* (New York: Harper & Row, 1958), pp. 142–45.

tain that both a human soul and the divine spirit were present in Christ. But this is only the beginning of the christological problem, not a solution. For how this is to be accomplished with philosophical integrity presents a most difficult puzzle. As we survey the history of Christian thought on this issue, we find that philosophical prolegomena was not only important, but even determinative for many of the solutions that were advanced. The great christological controversies that led up to the Council of Chalcedon were fueled to a large extent by the fact that early Christian thinkers came to the problem with different philosophical presuppositions, and consequently the quest for orthodoxy by those with one set of presuppositions was misunderstood as heresy by those with another set. The Platonists, centering around Alexandria, did not understand the Aristotelians; and the Aristotelian school, originating in Antioch and exerting great influence on Constantinople, was befuddled by the Platonists.[2]

For the Platonists, the heart of the puzzle was the question of how two spiritual entities, indwelling one body, could constitute one person, since it is the spiritual entity (i.e., the soul) that is the person. To put it differently, there are the human soul and the divine Word; how can these two natures together constitute one person? It was very easy for these thinkers to fall into the trap of positing a fusion of natures. Under this scheme (the heresy of Monophysitism, and especially its more extreme form, Eutychianism), Christ does not have two natures, a human one and a divine one, but one which represents an amalgam of both. Since, however, revelation attributes full humanity to Jesus as well as full deity, this solution was found to be unacceptable.

But the Aristotelians fared no better and committed heresies of their own. Under their presupposition of the unity of soul and body, it was difficult to see where the

2Ibid., pp. 310–43.

divine Word fit in. Since they did not think of the body as a container, no notion of two spiritual entities existing side by side in one body could be entertained. They had to conceive of the divine element as existing alongside the soul-body unit. The Aristotelians fell into the trap of deemphasizing any kind of unity between man and God in Christ. The heresy of Nestorianism posited a very weak link between the two on the level of the will of Christ. But this was insufficient to guard the integrity of the unity of the one person in Jesus Christ.

The definition of Chalcedon (A.D. 451) represents orthodoxy's attempt to compromise. It made binding the acceptance of one person with two natures, which are "without division or separation" (against the Nestorians) and "without confusion or change" (against the Monophysites). This formulation established clear guidelines for any further discussion and made recognition of heresy much easier. But to the philosopher it is a veritable nightmare. He is being asked to hold in balance two conceptions which appear to be logically contradictory and metaphysically impossible. No wonder that many people resigned themselves at this point to calling the whole matter a mystery and writing off any further attempts at speculation.

But the trouble with mysteries is that they remain and continue to baffle. Mysteries are not forgotten. They are puzzles crying out for a solution whenever the relevant facts are stated. Consequently, theological mysteries are not immune from the quest for philosophical clarity. The mystery of the incarnation, that is, the fact that God became man in Christ, is ontological. Epistemologically there is no hope of ever completely understanding the event, but that does not rule out philosophical inquiry into what the mystery is all about. In short, mystery or no, the questions persist and demand an answer.

## Models of Complementarity

If there is ever going to be a solution to the christological riddle, it must eliminate the idea that there is a contradiction in the union of the two natures. As long as they are seen as mutually exclusive, polar opposites, the hope for any understanding appears to be in vain. Of course, by means of a mystical way of thinking liberated from the obligations of logic and coherence, we could conclude that the two natures are noncontradictory. But a delight in ignorance and muddlement will certainly not advance the cause of understanding, so we will forego it as an option. Rather, we will analyze the components of divinity and humanity with an eye toward finding in their difference, not a contradiction, but complementarity.

Such an attempt was made by Thomas Aquinas. He provides a scheme for recognizing a positive relationship between man and God in Christ. His theory is referred to at times as a "subsistence" Christology. Aquinas states, "Let the Word be set down as *subsisting* in a human nature" (italics mine).[3]

Subsistence represents a unique metaphysical category. The conjunction of form and matter yields the existence of an essence as concrete substance. So the form of a vase, for example, conjoined to some clay, provides us with the existence of a vase. But this process occurs many times in a pottery factory, and each vase is a unique individual. This unique concrete instantiation is called the subsistence. For finite beings, such as man, subsistence is governed by material accidents which impinge on the otherwise pure essence. In God, who is not material, subsistence refers to the unique, independent presence of the divine person.

Aquinas applies the concept of subsistence to the rela-

---

[3]Thomas Aquinas, *Summa contra Gentiles*, trans. Charles J. O'Neil (Garden City, NY: Doubleday, 1957), vol. 4, p. 195.

tionship between humanity and deity in Christ.[4] By the term *subsistence* he indicates that here we have a unique instantiation of the divine person. "Existence" merely indicates that He is, but "subsistence" shows that He is *there* in a unique way compared with other forms of existence. By saying that in Christ God subsists in a human nature we are saying that here we have God in a unique incarnational mode.

This statement may not sound like much more than sophisticated question-begging. It smacks of answering the question of how the incarnation is possible by saying that it is possible incarnationally. No real answer has been given. But that is not Aquinas's intent; he goes on to elaborate on the nature of the subsistence.[5] Nonetheless, the minute the word *subsistence* is used, it becomes clear that we have a situation of complementarity, not exclusiveness. And that is a step in the right direction.

In explaining the nature of this subsistence, Aquinas delineates the particular ways in which the union could conceivably occur: on the level of nature, person, or accident. Union on the level of nature would imply a fusion of natures into one; this option has to be discarded as Monophysitism. Union by accident would really be no union at all; it would simply mean that a link which affects the essence of neither of the components (God and man) has been established. To give an example (not Aquinas's), neither a horse nor a cart is essentially affected by their being linked together; this would be a mere union of accidents. A union of accidents in Christ would be the Nestorian separation of natures. So the union must occur on the level of person. The two natures are united in the one person; thus we talk of the *hypostatic* (i.e., personal) union in Christ.[6]

Once again we must face up to the question of how this

[4]Ibid., pp. 193–97.
[5]Ibid., pp. 196–202.
[6]Ibid., pp. 193–95.

union is metaphysically conceivable. To continue with Aquinas's scheme, the most basic unity in a person with which we are familiar is that of matter and form, manifested as body and soul. This unity is inviolable if we want to maintain Christ's humanity. But there is another form of unity available, that between an instrument and its user. In many cases, such a unity is purely external and accidental, as between a man and the axe he uses. However, the union of a body part, say a hand, and the soul represents a unique internal instrumentality. It is not the unity of form and matter, for the soul is the form of the whole body, not just the hand. Still it is akin to that relationship, for the hand is directed and animated exclusively by the soul of the body to which it belongs.[7]

God stands to most men in a relation of external instrumentality. Though God uses people, there is no exclusive relationship between Him and them. But in the case of the one man, the incarnate Christ, there is a unique internal instrumentality. God has joined Himself to this one man in order to express Himself corporeally on earth.[8]

Christ, then, has a human nature, a unity of soul and body, based on the unity of form and matter. To this complex unit is joined a divine nature, with this unity being based on an exclusive internal instrumentality. Aquinas states that it is permissible to say "that the human nature is, so to speak, an instrument of the Word."[9] This instrumentality serves to perform God's work of redemption; but since we are here dealing with a real unity, it is not discarded as soon as the work of redemption is finished. The subsistence of the divine nature is then explained as God's assuming a human nature as a unique and exclusive instrument.[10]

This theory begins to reconcile the two natures, not in

[7]Ibid., pp. 195–97.
[8]Ibid., p. 198.
[9]Ibid., p. 197.
[10]Ibid.

the sense of amalgamating them, but by introducing a functional unity. Still, the problems have not been abolished. A functional unity presupposes a certain ontological complementarity. One cannot use a cloud of gas to hammer in a nail, and a toad cannot operate a construction crane. Yet we have expressed the difference between God and man not only in terms of disparity, but even edging toward the notion of opposition.

A contemporary effort to deal with this question is that of Karl Rahner.[11] He reminds us of a point made earlier in our discussion of man. We argued that it is part of the very nature of man to be disposed toward receptivity of the divine. Man may be finite and fall far short of the qualities of God. He is limited, whereas God is unlimited. But it is wrong to interpret this fact as an ontological contradiction. It is itself a shortcoming in man, but not an opposition. As much as man may be finite, his very being is directed to the infinite.

Rahner sees this very disposition of man to God, the *potentia obedientialis*, as man's most distinguishing characteristic.[12] If this be so, talk of contradiction and opposition within the hypostatic union must cease. In Christ, God has joined Himself to that which is already by its nature disposed to receiving Him. This is the epitome of what is possible with respect to fulfilling the potential. Jesus Christ is for Rahner the unique and highest instance of something which is potentially possible for all men. The incarnation is, then, not the height of paradox, but the height of fulfilment.[13]

Certain caveats are in order here. We must again re-

[11]Karl Rahner, "Jesus Christus, systematisch," in *Lexikon für Theologie und Kirche*, ed. J. Höfer and Karl Rahner (Freiburg: Herder, 1956–65), vol. 5, p. 956; *Foundations of Christian Faith*, trans. William V. Dych (New York: Seabury, 1978), pp. 192–203; "Current Problems in Christology," in *Theological Investigations*, trans. Cornelius Ernst (New York: Seabury, 1961), vol. 1, pp. 149–200.

[12]Karl Rahner, *Hearers of the Word* (New York: Seabury, 1969), p. 66.

[13]Rahner, "Jesus Christus," p. 956.

mind ourselves of the fallenness of man. Under our theological presuppositions, what Rahner says here can be accepted as referring to only ideal prefallen man or restored man. The disposition to receive God has been obscured in natural man by his misdirected will.

Further, we must not go beyond Rahner's own intentions and somehow see the incarnation as having been explained. The mystery, the ontological fact, is still there. All we have tried to do is to provide an underpinning of intelligibility to our concept of incarnation. Although we must be careful to observe these points of caution, we have achieved the goal of providing some categories for understanding the incarnation.

We can now observe that the models provided by Aquinas and by Rahner are not mutually exclusive. Aquinas approached the subject from the point of God who joins Himself to man as His instrument. Rahner starts at the point of man and shows that man is ready and waiting to be used by God in this way. There is an interplay between these two components, the subsistence of the divine and the *potentia obedientialis* of the human.

## The Trinity

What we have so far tried to show is that in this one person of Jesus Christ we see two natures, the human and divine. The humanity is shared with countless other men who each, in their own subsistence, enjoy the form of man along with particular accidents. But we must note that there is only one divine nature; it is found in the one God. This brings us to the problem of the Trinity. What philosophical concepts can help us understand that Jesus Christ is God, as is the Father, and as is the Holy Spirit, though there is only one God?

Probably no doctrine has been explored more in terms of its philosophical backgrounds than has the doctrine of the Trinity. Perhaps this is due to the fact that by all

accounts trinitarian formulations are essentially philosophical constructs. Whereas the Bible is certainly explicit on those elements that make up the Trinity, such as
the unity of God and the deity of Christ, the doctrine as
a whole is nowhere stated in the form in which most
Christians accept it. The doctrine represents a formula
which was developed by the church fathers to summarize
and draw together a set of biblical data difficult to reconcile. Consequently the philosophical components have
continually been the subject of discussion. In contrast to
the christological debates, where lack of philosophical
understanding was responsible for much unnecessary
disagreement, the trinitarian controversies were clearly
philosophically self-conscious. Because of the extensive
discussion that the philosophical background to the doctrine of the Trinity has received, what follows is largely
repetitive of what is said in most introductions to the
doctrine.[14]

Because the church fathers constructed the doctrine of
the Trinity in the framework of philosophical awareness,
we encounter a remarkable spirit of tolerance. On this
issue at least, they were by and large able to see beyond
philosophical nomenclature to the concepts.[15] We shall
follow this example as much as possible, though it makes
sense to be consistent with previously adopted terminol-

[14]For the development of the doctrine of the Trinity, see Kelly, *Early
Christian Doctrines*, pp. 83–137, 223–79.
[15]This is not to imply that there was not much discussion of terminology.
In fact there was; but whenever the discussion was long and protracted, even
concerning apparently small distinctions, the conceptual implications were
of great importance. Thus, for instance, the Nicene discussion on *homoou-
sion* versus *homoiousion* was a vital debate entailing the very deity of Christ,
not just an attempt at terminological nicety. The point is that whereas in
Christology the various philosophical camps simply did not understand each
others' language, to a great extent this difficulty was absent from the trinitarian controversies. Orthodox Platonists and Aristotelians fought side by
side against heretical conceptions. The debate was almost always substan-
tive, even when it was unproductive.

ogy. Further, we must be careful not to let terminological permissiveness allow conceptual muddiness.

## The Unity of God

The historical Christian witness is unanimous that there is one and only one God. From the outset, Christian apologists have insisted on the monotheistic nature of Christianity against the charges of tritheism. Even the trinitarian heresies erred almost exclusively on the side of overemphasizing the unity of God. Our question is how to understand this unity philosophically.

We earlier provided an argument for the uniqueness of God (pp. 126–27). This train of thought will apply here as well, of course. It is a clear safeguard against all deviations from monotheism, including tritheism. There cannot be more than one God.

Nonetheless, we covered only half the question with our previous argument. We showed that we cannot distribute deity equally over three beings. What remains is to demonstrate that there is an internal unity as well, that the deity of one being cannot be carved up to yield three thirds of a God.

This new task can be met by once again unpacking the philosophical conceptions we used to analyze any entity. We advanced the notion that the combination of form and matter endows a particular substance with being. Now this word *substance* has also come to be used frequently to express the unity of God. A second word, "essence," says roughly the same thing, but has a more abstract connotation. It would seem that "substance" is the better word here as it carries the connotation of an existent reality rather than an abstraction. For our purposes, the distinction is minimal though.

At this point there should be no question about the philosophical use of the term *substance*, even though it has several different meanings. A common usage of the term refers to the material or stuff of which something consists, as in "a gooey substance oozed out from under the door," or "the substance in the beaker is hydrochloric acid." But "substance" as it is used philosophically is not just the material cause of an entity. To follow Aristotle, "substance" is the unity of all causes: material, formal, final, and efficient.

We need also to distinguish this use of "substance" from its use in the writings of certain philosophers in the seventeenth and eighteenth century. For example, René Descartes in the *Meditations* describes his understanding of substance by means of an example involving a piece of wax.[16] We observe a piece of wax in its hardened state and note that it has a certain color, odor, texture, and so forth. Upon heating, the wax melts and all its properties change. Yet we still consider it to be the same wax. This is due, Descartes avers, to the fact that what actually makes this stuff wax is not any perceptible quality, but an underlying substance which can be perceived only through reason. Thus a substance is a substratum in which all the properties of an entity reside. But in our conception, a substance is the entire unity of an entity; and the essential properties, as determined by the form, are part and parcel of that entire unit.

Given this notion of substance, we see that there can be only one united divine substance. We have already argued that, since there is no way to individuate two supposedly divine substances, there cannot be two (or more) of them. But the idea of divine substance as a reservoir of deity into which different entities dip in order to be endowed with divine nature is also not possible. That would be tantamount to a strictly material conception of substance. Substance, on the contrary, refers to an entity as a whole; thus there cannot be more than one complete divine substance, and multiple entities cannot share this substance.

[16]René Descartes, *Meditations on First Philosophy*, trans. Donald A. Cress (Indianapolis: Hackett, 1979), pp. 20–23.

In short, there has to be a complete substance-entity identity in God. Hence, another way of referring to God's unity is to say that He is one Being. This is brought out by the fact that the word *ousia*, used by the Nicene fathers in this regard, can be translated "substance" or "being."

Let it be said, then, that the concept of God's unity excludes the idea that in the Trinity three beings are somehow combined into one. There is only one divine Being. When applied to God, terms such as "substance" and "essence" must be read as meaning this very thing. The concept of three beings becoming one (and vice versa) is illogical and unintelligible; it is most certainly not an intent of the trinitarian doctrine.

## *The Triadic Nature of God*

Having made this strong argument for the unity of God, we are now confronted with the puzzle that gave rise to the doctrine of the Trinity. Orthodox theologians agree that revelation predicates deity of the Father, the Son, and the Holy Spirit, and that, furthermore, these three stand in a relationship to each other that precludes their identity. Thus in the doctrine of God there is an element of threeness which does not seem to fit with our previous conclusions.

Once again there is a temptation to take flight into the notion of mystery as an escape. But what we said with regard to the mystery of the incarnation applies here as well. Epistemologically there is no hope of completely understanding the Trinity, but that does not preclude philosophical inquiry into what it is all about.

The resolution to the problem of unity and threeness cannot be found on the ontological level. There it is unimpeachable that there is one and only one divine Being. We must turn instead to the modalities of being. Here, as is well known, the theologian states that the one divine substance exists in three persons. This distinction is certainly helpful, and we must take recourse to some such terminology; but, unless more explanation is given, we are merely begging the question with an arbitrary terminological invention.

A being can exist in different modes. These modes can be rather different from each other, as we saw in Descartes's example of the piece of wax. The first step in constructing a trinitarian formulation is to recognize the possibility of a different mode for each of the three members of the Trinity. Then we can talk about God appearing in the mode of the Father, the Son, and the Spirit. The original expression of this series of modalities recalled the masks used in ancient drama (cf. Latin *persona*). God is said to be present at any time under one of these three masks.

This idea is both philosophically sound and theologically orthodox. But a problem comes up if no further qualifications are made; we would fall into the heresy that is variously known as modalism, Sabellianism, or patripassianism. The point of this heresy is that God expresses Himself through different modes at different times; but since He is one Being, He can assume only one mask at a time. There is no real distinction between the persons; it is always the one God who meets us under various guises. Theologically, modalism is repudiated on the basis of the biblical data which indicate a simultaneous distinction between the persons (e.g., Jesus praying to the Father) and which make a confusion of persons untenable (e.g., it was the Son and not the Father who suffered on the cross). Philosophically modalism complicates the issue tremendously.

The orthodox formulation requires us to posit three eternally distinct persons. The distinction of the three members of the Trinity is carried out on the level of person, not substance or being. But we still need to wrestle with the question of how this can be philosophically credible. It is one thing to say that we recognize this distinction in persons; it is another to make it more than an evasive formulation.

Recently there have been various attempts to deal with this question. Two particular insights ought to be mentioned.

1. Paul Tillich makes the point in his *Systematic Theology* that we may be wrong in setting up the Trinity as an object of theological exploration. After all, the doctrine itself is only a summary statement, a theological help in coming to a proper understanding of God. Tillich says that the medieval move to turn the Trinity into a "mystery to be adored" misses the point that the whole doctrine is an aid to understanding rather than data explicitly revealed as such in Scripture.[17] Tillich's warning is well taken. It is easy to get carried away in these philosophical explorations and start to apply transcendental criteria to what is already a transcendental category without realizing that this is what we are doing. We started out this discussion of the Trinity by saying that the Trinity itself is a philosophical concept, and, as such, is outside the range of theology. Hence we must remind ourselves that what we are doing is exploring the philosophical components of a philosophical construction.

Thus, with respect to the problem under consideration, we can say that, even though what we are doing is important, we are no longer working to facilitate theology. We did that by positing the notion of persons. We are now transcendentally facilitating the idea of "person" itself. Our work must go on, but only with the realization that theological coherence is not necessarily at stake. Therefore, we need not be alarmed if we cannot come up with a solution that answers all questions—as long as we are not left with some unintelligibility passed off as profundity.

2. Karl Rahner, in some ways relying on G. W. F. Hegel,

---

[17]Paul Tillich, *Systematic Theology* (Chicago: University of Chicago, 1963), vol. 3, p. 291.

shows that we may be able to penetrate beyond our rigid distinction between the members of the Trinity.[18] A theme which pervades his writings is that something becomes truly real only in conjunction with something other than itself. To give an example, Rahner says that a knower becomes one with his object of knowledge, and in the process of knowing finds himself.[19]

In an article on symbols, Rahner applies the same pattern to the Trinity.[20] Suppose a case where a symbol, $S$, stands for a reality, $R$. $R$ expresses itself through $S$. Thereby $S$ becomes $R$. But the basic reality of $R$ is not infringed upon; in fact, it is enhanced. The otherness of the symbol is genuine, and yet simultaneously it preserves the integrity of its referent.

Now the relation of the persons of the Trinity to the Godhead is somewhat like that of symbol to referent reality. The logic is the same, though this is not to say that the persons are merely symbolical. Instead of emphasizing the supposed incompatibility between the one substance and three persons, it may be more profitable to focus on their complementarity. The three persons are expressions of God, but this need not be seen as divisive. The unity and ontological integrity of God are enhanced, not threatened, by His existence in three persons.[21]

Rahner's point is helpful in understanding the Trinity. It need not detract from the ontological unity of God that there is a triad on the personal level. To infer any disunity would be a confused understanding. In fact, by emphasizing the three-personhood, we may also be adding credibility to the oneness of the Godhead.

But we still find ourselves in need of some metaphysical

[18]Cf. Winfried Corduan, "Hegel in Rahner: A Study in Philosophical Hermeneutics," *Harvard Theological Review* 71 (1978): 285–98.

[19]Karl Rahner, *Spirit in the World*, trans. William Dych (New York: Seabury, 1968), pp. 65–77.

[20]Karl Rahner, "The Theology of the Symbol," in *Theological Investigations*, trans. Kevin Smyth (New York: Seabury, 1966), vol. 4, pp. 221–52.

[21]Ibid., pp. 237–40.

categories under which to subsume the Trinity. Once again we turn to the notion of subsistence, which we already found beneficial in our discussion of the two natures of Christ (p. 153). We said then that subsistence is the particular concretization of an essence. Any particular essence can take on various forms of subsistence, depending on time and circumstance. Thus if we state that the three persons of the Trinity are three subsistences, we can account for the plurality of persons. There is more than one person because there is more than one subsistence.[22]

Of course we still have not accounted for the simultaneity of the three subsistences. It is easy to conceive of one being in three sequential subsistences; but when we talk of the three persons representing three mutually interacting subsistences at the same time, we are still faced with a serious problem. There are two points to keep in mind when we are faced with this problem:

1. No metaphysical system can do justice to the nature of God. Thus problems will always remain. But we must continue to work to improve our philosophical tools, never to be content with an inadequate metaphysics if it impairs theological understanding.

2. We must remember that temporal categories do not apply to God in Himself. Terms such as "sequential" and "simultaneous" reflect the temporality to which our experience is bound. But God is above that restriction. Thus the simultaneity of three subsistences is not a fatal stumbling block to our limited trinitarian prolegomena, though, admittedly, it does not make the matter easier to understand. We cannot think apart from temporal categories. This fact clouds our understanding of God's nature. All of our predications concerning His nature can be only analogical.

A further clarification needs to be added. We have used

[22]Cf. Thomas Aquinas: ". . . one must hold that in the divine nature three Persons *subsist*: the Father, the Son, and the Holy Spirit" (*Summa contra Gentiles*, vol. 4, p. 143—italics mine).

the concept of subsistence twice: with regard to Jesus Christ's divine nature indwelling His humanity, and with regard to the trinitarian persons. Are we then attributing two subsistences to Christ, one in the Godhead and one in His humanity? The answer is no; we are referring to the same subsistence. It is part of the subsistence of the second person of the Trinity to be incarnate.

# 10

# Regeneration

There is one final area to which we want to address our philosophical prolegomena. This concerns the work of redemption as it is applied to man. Thus we have come full circle. We began with man, turned to revelation, God, and Christ, and must now once again return to man as the focus of our discussion. Our final question is, What philosophical presuppositions are necessary for a proper understanding of man's salvation?

Whereas the previous chapter, the discussion of Christology, reflected a copious amount of previous philosophical thought, the topic in this chapter is usually left entirely to the theologian. What we are interested in particularly are the metaphysical aspects of regeneration. This is largely virgin territory when it comes to philosophical hermeneutics.

## Types of Changes in Man

A good work in systematics should be consulted for a discussion of all the changes on the anthropological level that accompany salvation.[1] Here it will suffice to outline

[1]Of course many such works abound. The reader's preference will be dictated by his confessional orientation. One of this writer's favorites is William G. T. Shedd, *Dogmatic Theology* (Grand Rapids: Zondervan, 1970 reprint), vol. 2, pp. 490–552.

three basic categories of change: ethical, positional, and ontological (metaphysical).

Ethical changes involve human actions. One of the great disputes in theology is, of course, about the extent to which the will is turned by God rather than functioning autonomously. In general, Arminians lean towards a freedom of the will to choose God and repent, whereas Calvinists put greater emphasis on the work of the Holy Spirit to incline the will to God and produce repentance as a fruit of His action. But neither side normally denies the ethical dimensions of salvation.

The ethical changes in salvation involve the will. Before redemption it was turned against God; now it is turned toward God. Consequently the human person now brings his life into line with God's ethical standards, certainly not to earn his salvation, but as part of the changes accompanying salvation.

Positional changes concern man's standing in relationship to God. To some extent, many of these can be understood forensically; justification, sanctification (in the root sense of "being set apart"), and adoption as sons may be included here. They provide a new basis for understanding the entire ethical dimension. It makes a great amount of difference whether the moral precepts of Scripture are understood from the vantage point of a rebel against God or of a justified son of God, for example. This distinction (as well as all ethical and positional changes for that matter) is grounded in metaphysical changes.

There are many Scripture passages indicating that there is a change in man's being upon redemption. "You must be born anew" (John 3:7). "If anyone is in Christ, he is a new creation" (II Cor. 5:17). "And I will give them a new heart, and put a new spirit within them; I will take the stony heart out of them and give them a heart of flesh" (Ezek. 11:19—unlike Ezek. 37, which refers to a revitalization of corporate Israel, this verse indicates a change within the individuals making up the nation).

All of these verses appear in a context which discusses either ethical or positional changes. But it would be wrong to understand them therefore as mere metaphors that describe ethical or positional changes. To the contrary, the invariable implication is that ethical and positional changes are facilitated because of metaphysical changes.

Titus 3:5b speaks of the "washing of regeneration and renewal of the Holy Spirit." This verse is clearly another reference to the same phenomenon of ontological change; the context contains a theological explication of the matter (vv. 5–8). First Paul makes a contrast between our inability to save ourselves and God's saving love to us. Then Paul states that this regenerative activity of the Holy Spirit, which God gave us through Jesus Christ, works toward our justification, which makes us heirs. Finally there is an exhortation to good deeds.

Thus we see in this passage a sequence of (1) ontological change (regeneration and renewal), (2) positional change (justification and inheritance), and (3) ethical change (good deeds). This sequence is probably not temporal; it may not even indicate a logical progression. But the point is clear that Paul here gives the metaphysical change a vital place in the whole work of redemption.

We see, then, that regeneration is an important aspect of the changes that occur when a man is saved. He becomes a new person. But how different is the new from the old? How can we say that he is still in any sense the same person? Can our earlier understanding of man account for this theological datum? We are in need of a philosophical hermeneutic for the doctrine of regeneration.

## Metaphysical Groundwork for Regeneration

The view of man which has determined this entire study has been that of a unity composed of a physical side and a spiritual side, matter and form. Form is what gives an entity its specific qualities and endows it with its being.

Clearly it is not the body which is changed in regeneration. The change has to take place in the form.

Up to this point we have very carelessly interchanged
terms such as "spirit," "soul," and "mind" to refer to the
form of man. There was no need to be more precise, and
it was convenient to interchange them. However, it is now
necessary to draw up some divisions in order to facilitate
understanding of our issue, regeneration. If the theologically inclined reader finds different terminology more appropriate, he may freely substitute his favorite words for
the ones we are using, just as long as the sense is preserved
or enhanced.[2]

### The Soul

Previously we described the form of man as his soul.
We want to retain this primary sense. The soul is what
makes a man a man; that is, it determines his humanity.
Of course his humanity assumes his animality. To clarify
what we mean by this, recall Aristotle's definition of man
as a "rational animal." In this definition both the genus
(animal) and the species (rational) as determined by the
form are included; after all, man is not pure rationality,
but an animal that is rational. In any event, even someone
who does not share Aristotle's concept has to say that one
of the most basic characteristics of man is the biological
nature which he shares with the animals.

Let us say, then, that this basic constitution of man's
form is most properly called his soul. As such, the soul
must carry out certain functions: (1) it gives life; that is,
it "animates" the individual; (2) it determines the nature
and arrangement of all basic biological processes; and (3)
it points man in the direction of rationality. Though the
soul, as we are now considering it, is not man's rationality, it makes man the kind of animal that has rational-

[2]Some of our use of nomenclature here relies on Robert Jewett, *Paul's
Use of Anthropological Terms* (Leiden: E. J. Brill, 1971).

ity. To cite an analogy: A bucket is not the water it contains, but the form which allows it to be filled with water. The actual rationality of man is located in his mind.

## The Mind

We attribute man's rationality itself to his mind. There is no need to reintroduce here the issue of materialism, the idea that man's mind is identical with his brain cells and processes; a purely materialistic view of the mind is clearly inadequate. In any event, the basic contention that man has a nonmaterial side must be broached at the point of a discussion of man's form in general. Man's mind is only a special case here, though the one which has drawn the most attention lately.

We can then agree at this point that man has a mind, and that this mind is not merely identical with his physiochemical brain events. Rather, his mind is an important aspect of his form (which of course means that it functions in continual conjunction with all the necessary physiological events of the brain). It is man's mind by which he thinks, conceptualizes, imagines, deliberates alternative courses of action, perceives outside information, and so forth.

## The Spirit

So far we have described two features of man's form which make him a different kind of an animal. But the next aspect to be discussed raises man high above the level of animals. This is man's spirit. Man's spirit determines that faculty of his which establishes a relationship with God. This is not to say that the spirit is the relationship, or merely the capacity for the relationship, but the spirit is the ontologically real part of the form of man whose function it is to facilitate that relationship.

It is the possession of a spirit which makes man unique. He occupies a place where the realms of the material and the spiritual meet, containing both qualities in himself.

Having a spirit does not make man divine, but it gives him a capacity for communion with the divine such as no other material creature possesses.

In man's spirit dwells the *imago Dei*, the image of God shared by all humans. It is precisely in his spirituality that man most resembles God, though we must be careful in our understanding of this. Let us remember that we are here talking about form, not substance. Thus we are not isolating an entity superimposed on man, as though it were another, albeit spiritual, organ added to his anatomy. Rather, this spirituality, the image of God, is expressed (as form to matter) through man's outward inclinations, namely, his morality, rationality, and even religiosity. As spirit is part of the form of man, it determines all of his being. Hence man as a whole expresses the image of God, but the source of this expression is localized in his spirit.

We see, then, that man's spirit and his will are intimately related. The will, as part of the total man, is directed by the spirit in that the spirit supplies the will with the necessary capacities for its activities. At the same time, the spirit is also directed by the will in that the spirit is either open towards God or closed to Him. Consequently, if either will or spirit breaks down (i.e., does not function as intended by the Creator), the other faculty is hurt as well, and the total man is affected.

A similar, but somewhat looser, relationship exists between the spirit and the mind. The spirit directs the mind, frequently by means of the will, to be either in tune or out of tune with God. But the mind also influences the spirit. It can feed the spirit by assimilating proper material, or it can cause the spirit to shrivel by misuse or underuse.

There are other anthropological terms important in Scripture, for example, "conscience" and "heart." As this is not intended to be a biblical theology, let it suffice for purposes of clarity to say that these are metaphorically expressed (to varying degrees) functions of the spirit of man. An interesting sidelight is provided by the fact that the word *flesh*, as it is sometimes used by the apostle Paul, refers, not to the physical side of man, but to a part of his spirituality, namely, man's desire for self-sufficiency.[3]

We have broken down the form of man into three components: soul, mind, and spirit. No doubt further detailed categorizations are possible and desirable. But our scheme is now sufficient for our purposes in this chapter.

## Corruption

In chapter 4 we argued that the fall of man was in principle a misdirection of the will. We stated further that this misdirection did not affect the intellectual capacity of the mind; essentially the misdirection only sent the mind astray from God. But this is not to say that there are no other metaphysical changes as a result of the fall.

The fall occurred when man decided by his will to disobey God and serve himself. Man wanted to be his own god and do what was right in his eyes rather than submit to God's will. The disparity in wills was not confined to this first instant, however, but has become the continual habit of man. How can this be? Clearly something happened within man himself that permanently altered his structure so as to leave the will bent away from God once it had assumed that direction.

Where in man did this change occur? First of all, there seems to be no indication in Scripture that man's physical nature was changed. Man's soul was not altered either. Immortality is not an essential property of man which was changed after the fall. The Bible teaches (I Tim. 6:16) that immortality is an essential property of God alone. All

[3]E.g., in Gal. 3:3, where Paul makes the distinction between relying on God's Spirit or on flesh, that is, the works of the law.

other beings that are immortal are so only by God's act. The mortality of man is a result of God's withholding His power of support. Thus we must look for the internal change in man elsewhere.

We have already mentioned that since the fall the mind's stance toward God has been adversely affected by the misdirection of the will. Moreover, this is a two-way street, for the will acts on the information presented to it by the mind. If the mind gives the will information biased against God, chances are the will is going to exercise itself against God. However, the unreliability of the mind is not enough to explain the continual disinclination of the will. For this we have to look to a deeper level.

In the last section we postulated an intimate relationship between the will and the spirit and their mutual interdependence. The spirit is the one aspect of man which will be devastated by a failure on the part of the will. And once the spirit, the ontological basis for the will, has been corrupted, it is easy to see how the will cannot straighten itself out again. The will has, so to speak, pulled the ontological rug out from under itself; and, having once slipped, it cannot return itself to firm footing.

This point is one frequently missed by theological analysts. For example, Thomas Aquinas understands the corruption of human nature as essentially a disjointedness between the rational soul and the will, a disjointedness which can be righted (only by God's grace, to be sure) by a renewed coordination between these two faculties.[4] But this point of view misses the severity of the corruption; once the will went awry, the spirit broke as well.

[4]"Natural good is corrupted, inasmuch as man's nature is disordered because man's will is not subject to God's and when this order is overthrown, the consequence is that the whole nature of sinful man is disordered. . . . The order of nature can be restored, *i.e.*, man's will can be subject to God, only when God draws man's will to Himself" (Thomas Aquinas, *Summa Theologica*, I–II, q. 109, art. 7, in *Introduction to St. Thomas Aquinas*, trans. and ed. Anton C. Pegis [New York: Modern Library, 1945], pp. 664–65).

We have argued that the spirit is one aspect of the total form of man. So, now speaking in general terms, it is not possible for the spirit to become deformed without misshaping the form as a whole. And this effect implies, of course, that the deformity stretches itself over all of man's being with the possibility of secondary effects on the physical and animal levels. Thus all of man is in a fallen state; the entire race has become degenerate as well. Man after the fall is not merely prefall man with a flaw; he is, to use the appropriate theological jargon, totally depraved.

All of this is not to deny that man is still a spiritual creature. The spirit is still there. It still bears the imprint of the image of God. Man still has a spiritual capacity yearning to be fulfilled. Nonetheless, under the influence of the fall the spirit is incapable of proper fulfilment of its intended potential. Man, we read in Romans 1, having turned from God, falls into idolatry, futility of mind, and moral decay.

## Regeneration

It is now obvious why the doctrine of regeneration is so important. The full redemption of man requires that the metaphysical destruction resulting from the fall be taken care of. Unless man's spirit is renewed, man's will can never be in accord with God's will again, except by occasional accident.

The sequence of regeneration is the opposite from corruption. In the fall, man's will affected the spirit. Now in the restoration, the spirit must first (logically if not temporally) be brought back to integrity, and then the rectification of the will can follow.

This ontological dimension to the doctrine of regeneration is frequently missed. As pointed out already, Aquinas thought of the process as merely one of realignment of soul and will. Calvin speaks of a renewal of the will, but does not emphasize a previous reconstitution of man's spirit.[5] However, our discussion should have made it clear by now that the ontological renewal is not only scriptural, but also makes good philosophical sense.

But there are further theological data with which this philosophical description must come to terms. For the Scriptures do not speak of a repair or patching up of man's spirit; the imagery is consistently one of complete renewal. Man's spirit is replaced by a new spirit; he receives a new heart. So this entire aspect of man's form is renewed. This is a startling observation and has some important consequences.

1. If the spirit is changed, the form is changed. But if the form is changed, the whole man is changed. Thus, next, man's will is renewed. He can now exercise it freely toward God. We see here the reversal of the process involved in the fall of man. But since the spirit is new, and not just the old one made over, the product is not just a restoration of prefall man; we have here a brand new being, literally, a new man. The change in the spirit may, via mediate causes, bring about changes in behavior, thinking, and possibly even bodily appetites or dispositions.

Now it is clear that not all of the effects are realized immediately upon the initial point of regeneration. This fact has caused some theologians to think of regeneration as a long process rather than an instantaneous event. But philosophically it presents no difficulty. It is not necessary for all the effects of a form to be realized immediately. The form actualizes whatever potential is given to it, but this actualization may take a while. The form, nonetheless, is complete.

An illustration may make this point clearer. A human infant is to be considered fully human. Some thinkers

---

[5]John Calvin, *Institutes of the Christian Religion*, 3. 3, ed. John T. McNeill (Philadelphia: Westminster, 1960), pp. 592–621.

would consider a fetus only potentially human,[6] but this restriction does not apply to the baby after birth. It fully possesses the form of humanity, yet many essential properties of humanity do not appear in the child until relatively late in life. These properties include the ability to reproduce other humans and the full exercise of reasoning powers. Even though these properties are already entailed in the form of man, at first they are potential only. It takes a while for all of them to become actualized.

Similarly at the point of re-creation (the new birth) man receives a new spirit, thereby re-creating his entire form. But it may take a very long time before all the potential of the new form has totally transformed all of his mind, body, soul, and will. For most believers, one suspects, this process takes at least a lifetime. Thus our philosophical model allows for a punctiliar understanding of regeneration while not undermining a process view of sanctification. Further, the theologian who prefers a concept of crisis sanctification can, by way of this model, still distinguish between regeneration and sanctification, allowing for the latter's occurrence at a later point in time. Regardless of one's theological position on the time of sanctification, it has to be seen as the actualization of the new nature (determined by the form) as it is present within the Christian.

2. Another characteristic of the new spirit within regenerate man is its close conjunction with the Holy Spirit of God. Scripture records a large number of activities which God's Spirit, dwelling within man, carries out with or through man's spirit.[7] Thus there appears to be a genuine relationship between the two spirits. It would no doubt be going too far to postulate any kind of ontological identification here; even the concept of subsistence seems too strong. Man and God are not and cannot be commen-

---

[6]E.g., Norman L. Geisler, *Ethics: Alternatives and Issues* (Grand Rapids: Zondervan, 1971), pp. 218–19.

[7]Rom. 8:14, 26; Gal. 5:22–25; Eph. 1:13; I John 4:13, etc.

surate to this extent except in Christ's incarnation. At the
same time, we ought not to underplay the reality of this
conjunction. God the Spirit indwells man and quickens
man's spirit, directs him, prays with him, and so on. All
who are regenerate are indwelt in this way.[8]

To understand this relationship, we need to strike a
proper balance between division and conjunction. The
notion of indwelling makes it clear that we are not dealing
with an occasional relationship. At the same time, we
know that it is possible for man's spirit to quench the
Holy Spirit at times.[9] Regardless of how one interprets
that phrase, it is clear at least that even regenerate man
is not continually bound in his will to the will of the Holy
Spirit. Thus, technically the relationship is not a necessary one.

Once again we take recourse to the concept of the *potentia obedientialis*. Man by nature is directed to God and
His revelation. If this capacity is present in unregenerate
man, we can posit its existence in a new and improved
form in the new spirit *a fortiori*. We can then visualize the
relationship between man's spirit and God's Spirit as a
fuller actualization of this *potentia*. Of course we must
differentiate between this fulfilment of the *potentia obedientialis* and the supreme fulfilment it received in the
incarnation of God in Jesus Christ. Though some of the
same metaphysical categories may apply, we are obviously not here dealing with the identity that we see
between the Spirit and Christ. Man's *potentia* is of a far
lesser nature, both qualitatively and quantitatively. Nonetheless, it is a real conjunction of the two kinds of spirit,
a conjunction which will be even further actualized in the
next life.

[8]The counterpositive of Rom. 8:9b, "If anyone does not have the Spirit of
Christ, he does not belong to Him" (NASB), is, "If anyone does belong to
Christ, he has His Spirit." Thus the only requirement Scripture places on
anyone's possessing the Spirit is to be born again.

[9]I Thess. 5:19.

In this final chapter we have searched for some philosophical categories to understand the work of redemption, particularly regeneration. This endeavor rounds out our prolegomena. We began with man and have ended with man, providing philosophical categories which make it possible to have a greater understanding of the theological environment into which God has placed him.

## For Further Reading

The following brief list may be helpful for further understanding of the relationship between philosophy and theology. Not all of these works are referred to in the text.

Augustine. *Confessions.* Trans. John K. Ryan. Garden City, NY: Doubleday, 1960.

Barth, Karl. *Die protestantische Theologie im 19. Jahrhundert.* Zürich: Evangelischer, 1952.

Geisler, Norman L., ed. *Biblical Errancy: An Analysis of Its Philosophical Roots.* Grand Rapids: Zondervan, 1981.

Jüngel, Eberhard. *Gottes Sein ist im Werden.* Tübingen: Mohr, 1965.

Kelly, John N. D. *Early Christian Doctrines.* New York: Harper & Row, 1958.

Küng, Hans. *Menschwerdung Gottes.* Freiburg: Herder, 1970.

Metz, Johannes Baptist. *Christliche Anthropozentrik.* Munich: Kösel, 1962.

Rahner, Karl. *Hearers of the Word.* Trans. Michael Richards. New York: Seabury, 1969.

Thomas Aquinas: *Summa contra Gentiles.* 4 vols. Garden City, NY: Doubleday, 1957.

# Index

181